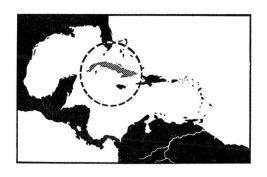

CARIBBEAN SERIES, 7

Sidney W. Mintz, Editor

SUGAR AND SOCIETY IN THE CARIBBEAN

An Economic History of Cuban Agriculture

by Ramiro Guerra y Sánchez
with an Appendix by José Antonio Guerra y Debén
Foreword by Sidney W. Mintz

New Haven and London, Yale University Press, 1964

Copyright © 1964 by Yale University.
Designed by Sally Hargrove,
set in Times Roman type,
and printed in the United States of America by
The Carl Purington Rollins Printing-Office
of the Yale University Press.
Translated from the Spanish by Marjory M. Urquidi.

Library of Congress catalog card number: 63–13962

Published with assistance from
the Rockefeller Foundation,
whose grant made the translation possible.

It is a natural law that a people who surrender the cultivation of their land to others abdicate all lawful ownership; uprooted and without a future, their lives become no more than transient incidents in human history.—*Report of the Cuban Commissioners to the Information Board in 1866. Proposal on Immigration made by Francisco de Frías, Count of Pozos Dulces.*

To the memory of my father

Contents

Foreword

by Sidney W. Mintz

In this book about men and sugar, Dr. Ramiro Guerra recounts a history. His story is laid in the Caribbean islands—islands which, for most of us, did not even exist a decade ago. Dr. Guerra purports to demonstrate that in these islands men and sugar were long ago drawn into remarkably patterned relationships, and that all of these relationships have developed along some parallel course or trajectory. This is history—social, political, and economic history—and it aspires to be generalizing; its author means to locate sociological regularities within bodies of historical fact.

Dr. Guerra's book was published for the first time in 1927, and he did not change it substantially in later (1935, 1944) editions, except to make some few additions. The original materials had appeared first as a series of newspaper articles, which is reflected in the fact that the book consists of many brief chapters. In preparing this English version, considerable cutting was done: the prefaces to the second and third editions, many footnotes (especially to the later editions), appendices, and portions of the text have been removed, in order to avoid repetition. The final product is shorter than the original, but everything possible was done to maintain textual continuity and to cleave to the original intent of the author.

Since 1927, some of Dr. Guerra's predictions have come true; as one reads, one is made to feel that the author had a firm sense of the future as he wrote. And yet it was to the past that he turned for insight. He produces for us, right at the start, a brief drama of economic and demographic history: the seventeenth-century transformation of a flourishing yeoman agricultural colony (Barbados) into one enormous socially degraded plantation. And then he helps us to understand why this tragic drama has repeated itself again and again, sometimes with explosive consequences, in the Caribbean. When Dr. Guerra turns to the history of his own country, Cuba, we find portent in his words.

The translation and republication of this book, then, is more than an exercise in intellectual history. It is true that, even were Dr. Guerra's analysis of no relevance to today's events, his book would still be significant for the way it expresses the social values of the Cuban scholarly community of the post-World War I years. But that in its assertions we can find an eerie pointer to a future now past enhances its value as a historical and social science document.

The Caribbean islands, or Antilles, stretch in a great arc from Cuba and Jamaica in the northwest to Trinidad, off Venezuela, in the southeast. Together with the Central American coast, they ring that sea which got its name from the Island-Carib (Galibi) Indians who once lived in the smaller islands, the Lesser Antilles. The Greater Antilles—Cuba, Jamaica, Hispaniola (today's Haiti and Santo Domingo), and Puerto Rico— are arrayed from west to east. Off Puerto Rico's eastern tip, the Lesser Antilles begin and curve southward: the U.S. and British Virgin Islands; the so-called Leewards and Windwards; Tobago, and Trinidad; and the offshore islands of the northern coast of South America.

In all, some hundreds of islands, occupied by perhaps fifteen million people, five sovereign political units, and scores of islands under the political control or administration of other powers—this was the heritage of 450 grim years of colonial authority. The islands are mostly mountainous, but their coastal plains are very suitable for tropical agriculture; the settings and the climate (in spite of hurricanes and volcanoes) are benign.

Spain was first in Europe to the islands and swiftly established colonies in Hispaniola, Cuba, Puerto Rico, and Jamaica. Spanish military action, enslavement of war prisoners, and disease substantially destroyed the aboriginal population of those islands. At the same time, Spain introduced the sugar cane, African slaves, and the plantation to the Antilles. Fernando Ortiz and Mervyn Ratekin,[1] and Dr. Guerra himself, tell us of

1. Fernando Ortiz, *Cuban Counterpoint* (New York, Knopf, 1947), pp. 254–82; Mervyn Ratekin, "The Early Sugar Industry in Española," *Hispanic American Historical Review, 34,* February 1953, 1–20.

these early experiments in plantation agriculture, which, after initial failures, proved successful.

The organization of plantations based on forced labor may seem to have been a "natural" or "expectable" accompaniment to the economic development of the New World. But there was nothing either natural or expectable about it; from the perspective of post-Roman European history, the plantation was an absolutely unprecedented social, economic, and political institution, and by no means simply an innovation in the organization of agriculture. Large-scale demand for certain staples, particularly on the part of the consumers and the new industries of Old World cities, brought the plantation into being; newly discovered territories, where land was a gift or readily acquired booty—the Antilles, and the Atlantic coast from Virginia to Brazil —provided it with a setting. But the plantation's needs for labor, as it turned out, had to be satisfied by force. The history of newly discovered and newly occupied areas has demonstrated again and again that free men will not work as employed agricultural laborers if they have access to land which they can cultivate for themselves.

Basic to the relationship between men and land, then, is the relative availability of land for settlement and of labor for employment. In areas of sparse settlement, free men will settle unoccupied and unappropriated land and avoid working for others—what Nieboer called "open resources."[2] It is precisely the ease with which land may be acquired in such situations that makes employable labor "scarce." Contrariwise, in

2. H. J. Nieboer, *Slavery as an Industrial System* (The Hague, Martinus Nijhoff, 1900), pp. 420–22.

areas where settlement is dense—or can swiftly be made dense by massive immigration—and where land has been taken up and converted into somebody's property, *rentiers* can garner a profit in the form of rent, and entrepreneurs can profitably employ wage earners at the then-prevailing market price of labor. This is Nieboer's situation of "closed resources." The contrast, Edgar Thompson says,[3] consists in that in one case, two would-be employers chase one laborer; in the other, two would-be laborers chase one employer. Since the Caribbean islands were "open" in the period of early settlement, the European settlers who wished to establish plantations there and to engage labor had no solution to their labor problems but the use of bonded and enslaved men. The plantation, then, was a pioneer institution at first and needed a coerced labor force because it could not amass or retain a free labor force.

But the early plantations of the Hispanic settlements flourished only briefly. The discovery of mainland riches in labor and precious metals distracted the Crown and the colonists, and the sturdy Caribbean colonies of Spain were losing ground, rather than gaining, by the third decade of the sixteenth century. The slowed rate of growth of these colonies—Hispaniola, Cuba, Puerto Rico, and Jamaica—was caused in part by depopulation and the loss of imperial interest. But it also resulted from the arbitrary mercantilist policies of the Crown. In this respect, Spain differed from her northern enemies. The uneven and chronically feeble developmental efforts Spain made or permitted in her Antillean colonies between the early sixteenth and mid-eighteenth

3. Edgar Thompson, "The Plantation" (unpublished dissertation, University of Chicago, 1932).

centuries gave to those colonies an odd tranquility in the midst of war and plunder. Though they were attacked repeatedly, and though Britain seized Jamaica (1655) and France acquired part of Hispaniola (1697), the rest of the Hispanic Caribbean (eastern Hispaniola, Puerto Rico, and Cuba) meanwhile took on a distinctive identity over the course of more than two centuries of slowed development. Among the collateral effects of economic isolation were the growth of relatively unstratified societies, the emergence of extremely liberal slavery codes, and the multiplication of the free population of color—all developments which set these colonies apart from those of Spain's rivals at a later time.

The first non-Hispanic European settlements in the Antilles were not slave plantations; they were communities of free-born farmers, or of indentured servants who eventually earned their freedom and became yeomen. The conversion of such communities into great slave plantations was accomplished with remarkable rapidity, once the slave trade expanded, the European markets for plantation staples were secured, and the capital to establish plantation enterprises was forthcoming. But the human cost was very high. It was paid, first of all, by the yeoman farmers themselves, driven from island to island in their search for land they could hold against the spreading plantation. It was paid, secondly, by the African slaves.

The plantation system which extirpated the yeoman farmers of the non-Hispanic Antilles and scourged West Africa for centuries richly rewarded its organizers. The wealth produced by African slaves on land wrested from Arawak and Carib Indians flowed into the European metropolises in great rivers, nourishing infant industry, making possible the foundation of great families, and supporting the growth and spread of culture and civilization in the form of universities, libraries, museums, and symphony orchestras. Plantation products also did their part for Western civilization. West Indian tobacco, coffee, sugar, and rum, together with Indian tea, were effective fare for the factory workers of Britain and France, quelling their hunger pangs and numbing their outrage.

Slave plantations in the Caribbean islands producing sugar for European markets were established by Spain's enemies in the latter decades of the first half of the seventeenth century, first by Britain in Barbados. On that island, as Dr. Guerra demonstrates, the classic pattern of plantation growth was revealed: original settlement by yeoman colonists; destruction of the yeoman community by massive African slave importations and of yeoman agriculture by plantation growth; market crisis as new competitors appeared (sometimes followed by the collapse of local plantation enterprise); and finally, slave emancipation or revolution. The various European powers who established plantation colonies in the Antilles arranged their dealings with the planter class on mercantilist terms—they aimed at monopolizing both the product and the buying power of their colonials. But when several islands of the same power (e.g. Britain's Barbados and Jamaica) produced the same commodity (such as sugar), they inevitably competed, at least with each other. And when a rival power opened up plantation production on a new island and on an enlarged scale—as France did after 1697, when it wrested Haiti (St. Domingue) from Spain by war and treaty—its cheaper sugars intensified political difficulties between the rival colonies and their respective metropolises.

The slave plantation economy, so rich and promising an avenue for investment, made great fortunes for many at home; it bankrupted many as well. For one thing, the opening of new lands by war and politics could glut a well-established market; thus the conquest of Jamaica enriched new planters, while bankrupting those in Barbados. For another, slave revolts and military operations by a powerful enemy could wreck a prosperous colony, as the revolution in St. Domingue wrecked that colony for France. Ill-used land, maltreated labor, jealous enemies, and the fortunes of war —these were the elements from which great wealth could be amassed, indeed, but the plantation economy was speculative by any reasonable long-term judgment. In the history of the Caribbean sugar plantations from the 1640s to the early nineteenth century, colony supplanted colony, power succeeded power, in tragic succession.

The nineteenth century witnessed enormous changes within the Caribbean area. The Haitian revolution, which had begun in the last decade of the eighteenth century, came to a bitter close, and Haiti became the New World's second sovereign state. In Napoleonic Europe, the discovery of effective means for the processing of beet sugar raised another specter besides revolution to haunt the planters. The slave trade, country by country, was gradually outlawed. Finally, slavery itself ended—for the Dutch, the English, the French— by 1860, only Spain and Brazil (and the United States, of course) were slaveholding powers in this hemisphere.

Technical advances in the Caribbean sugar industry in the nineteenth century came about largely as a result of steam power, which was introduced in some parts of the Caribbean in the early decades of the century. Some areas lagged behind, letting tariff protection, fresh lands, slave labor, or curtailed earnings take the place of technical improvement. During the nineteenth century, the range of variation in scale of operation, technical level, degree of capitalization, and productivity in Caribbean sugar production grew wider. In some places, raw brown sugar "cones" or "heads" were still processed for local use or sale in country market places, by methods which had remained essentially unchanged for several centuries. Yet by the 1880s the same colony or country might possess modernized plantations producing cane on 1,000 acres of land and grinding thousands of tons each harvest in their respective mills.

Growth of the large plantations was accompanied by increasing mechanization of the field operations, greater grinding capacities for individual mills, and growing rationalization of production. At the same time, the older and more conservative mills fell further behind, keeping their now-outdated machinery intact, and preserving the same productive levels. The widening gap between the more "progressive" and more "conservative" mills was enlarged still further by abolition. Where labor was relatively scarce—that is, in areas where land could still be acquired by free men—the economically more marginal plantations were often pushed out of production. The larger, more mechanized enterprises reorganized themselves on the basis of free or contract labor and held on. The total effect was the elimination of the smaller, less successful, less mechanized plantations, though in some colonial situations they were artificially protected for a longer period than in others.

At the same time, the decline of the "classic" small-scale slave plantation and the emergence of sovereign Haiti and Santo Domingo produced an interesting social and agricultural countertrend: the vigorous emergence of classes of small-scale landholders who produced some items for world markets and others for their own consumption and for local exchange. Such peasants—the word here is used to describe folk who live by just such an economic adaptation—harked back in some ways to the early yeomen of the Antilles, those social groups which were driven out by the plantations or had survived feebly on the margins of society. The new peasantries took shape on the peripheries of the plantation areas, starting small farms on the lands of ruined plantations, as in Jamaica, and spreading over the mountainous interior, as in Haiti; growing tobacco, coffee, nutmegs, arrowroot, and similar tropical products in the out-of-the-way areas of all those islands where slavery had ended and land could somehow be had.

Such "reconstituted peasantries"[4] developed, in many cases, alongside the lowland plantations. They represented a reaction to the plantation economy, a negative reflex to enslavement, mass production, monocrop dependence, and metropolitan control. Though these peasants often continued to work part-time on plan-

4. S. W. Mintz, "The Question of Caribbean Peasantries: A Comment," *Caribbean Studies, 1,* October 1961, pp. 31–34.

tations for wages, to eke out their cash needs, their orientation was in fact antagonistic to the plantation rationale. Thus, in the Caribbean colonies of The Netherlands, France, and Britain, a whole new way of life grew, largely in the interstices between plantation areas. Many of these people were of African origin, as in Haiti and Jamaica; others were descendants of East Indian, Javanese, Portuguese, Canary Island, Yucatecan, or Chinese contract laborers who had been brought to the islands in the post-Emancipation years to push down the local cost of plantation labor and to weaken the independent spirit of the ex-slaves. In each sovereign country or colony, the local agricultural adaptation was elaborated, often as some mutual accommodation of plantation and peasant agriculture.

But the last islands to participate in this historical succession, this patterned sequence of plantation and peasantry, were two of the last New World possessions of Spain: Puerto Rico and Cuba. Thus the Hispanic Caribbean came to represent a final chapter and a capstone in the plantation cycle.

That the Hispanic islands lay largely outside this panorama is one of the quirks of Caribbean history. We have seen that they were the first to plant the sugar cane; the first to have slaves; the first to undertake the organization of slave-operated plantations. And yet the infant Hispaniolan, Puerto Rican, and Cuban sugar industries of the early 1500s stagnated, and the epic of the slave plantation was left for the British, the Dutch, the French, the Danes, and others to write much later. Only when those nations had already begun to turn away from the plantation economy did the Hispanic islands stir once more.

In Cuba the renewed period of plantation growth began in the middle of the eighteenth century. Later, the Haitian revolution, wiping out as it did the richest sugar-producing colony of all, stimulated the growth of the plantation system in Cuba and Puerto Rico (though not in Spanish Hispaniola itself), and launched them on the path taken by their Dutch, English, French, and other predecessors.

Yet there were important differences, especially in the case of Cuba. By the time the plantation system began to expand in Cuba, that colony had a society, a people, and a culture of its own. We have seen that, for over two centuries, Cuba was able to build its society slowly, without protracted disturbance from the outside, and to avoid the plantation mode of development. One can justly refer to the growth of a "creole adaptation"[5] in the Cuban setting. The economy rested heavily on small-scale agriculture (some of the products of which, such as tobacco and coffee, were processed and exported) and on livestock-raising (which provided food as well as export items such as hides and tallow).

The appearance and success of large numbers of substantially self-sufficient cultivators and small-scale peasant producers over the centuries was almost unique in the Caribbean; the other Hispanic colonies in the Antilles, Santo Domingo (till 1844) and Puerto Rico, most resembled Cuba in this regard. Though there were periods of isolation, and attempted invasions by other powers (Britain, for instance, occupied Havana for some months in 1763–64), Cuban society gradually

5. The term is used here in one sense—someone (or something) of Old World origins, but born in the colony. The descendants of the Spanish immigrants to Cuba were, then, Creoles.

took on a special quality: rural in emphasis, anti-Spanish but pro-Hispanic, folk-Catholic, creole. As the country developed a distinctive literature, music, dialect of Spanish, and national ideology, it acquired cultural integrity and solidarity as well.

Also contributing to the development of a distinctively Cuban society was the fact that, from the start of the sixteenth century until the middle of the eighteenth, the slave population of the island was provided with ample opportunities to become free. Spanish law, Catholicism, the slow rate of economic growth, and Iberian racial attitudes conspired to help the freedmen to integrate themselves in Cuban life swiftly and thoroughly. The percentage of Cuba's population which was of slave status was low at any point in the island's history, but it was particularly low before the 1760s. The contrast with the Antillean colonies of Britain, France, and The Netherlands was striking. Cuba was predominantly European in culture, but creolized; its population, both white and colored, lived mainly by independent farming and grazing, and its slaves were few. The colonies of other powers were, for the most part, populated by masses of slaves without any hope of improving their condition, and the only Europeans who inhabited these plantation settlements were overseers, government officials, and adventurers.

Cuba's near-uniqueness rested in her cultural synthesis, in the economic independence of her people, and in the protection she was provided against the spread of the plantation system. But the price of this protection and isolation was subjection to the imperial arbitrariness of the metropolis. It was Cuba's subsequent struggle in the 1860s and 1870s for political and cultural autonomy from Spain which gave her the focus she needed to become a cohesive nation. Cuba as a Spanish colony had more nationhood than the colonies of the other European powers in the Antilles might have had as sovereign states.

It is because of this cultural integrity that Dr. Guerra, in his description of the spread of the plantation system in Cuba from the closing decades of the eighteenth century onward, assumes what some might regard as an unusually benign and undisturbed view of what happened. The fact is that the onrush of the plantation cycle made important changes in Cuban life, many of them malevolent. The intensification of slavery and the slave trade damaged civil liberties and increased the legal and social persecution of the slaves. The deterioration of civil liberties in Cuba was accompanied by an improvement in the economic situation of the country as a whole. Sugar and slavery might have boded ill for the rural poor; but they meant prosperity and expanded opportunity for the large-scale landowners. Somewhat ironically, Cuba's intensified plantation orientation developed precisely as the British and French West Indian colonies were disengaging themselves from this orientation.[6] One famous student of colonialism could write, in the early nineteenth century, that the Spanish Antilles had been commonwealths when the British Antilles were factories; now, he continued, the Spanish islands were becoming factories, while he hoped that the British islands would soon be commonwealths.[7]

6. S. W. Mintz, "Labor and Sugar in Puerto Rico and Jamaica," *Comparative Studies in Society and History, 1,* March 1959, pp. 273–83.

7. H. Merivale, *Lectures on Colonization and Colonies* (London, Longman, 1841), p. 39.

Cuba's push toward sovereignty was complicated by plantation prosperity and by the revival of the slavery issue. Spain had agreed (under British pressure) to outlaw the trade, but slaves continued to pour into Puerto Rico and Cuba. Slavery was not terminated until 1873 (or 1876, to mark the end of apprenticeship) in Puerto Rico, and until 1880 (1886) in Cuba; and slaves were transported illegally to these islands almost up to the moment of Emancipation. The last half-century of the trade—legally terminated by treaty in 1820, but continuing for about fifty years thereafter—probably added at least 200,000 slaves to the island population. So immense an increase (the population in 1877 was slightly more than a million and a half), even in a society with as much identity and shape as Cuba's, inevitably produced strains in the social system. One of Cuba's great historians, José Antonio Saco, was concerned with the "blackening" of Cuba's population. In fact, the physical type of the newcomers was irrelevant, except for what people might make of the difference. What mattered were the cultural differences and, most of all, the differences in status, between free native-born Cubans and the masses of enslaved, illiterate, newly arrived, and unacculturated migrants.

The apogee and gradual decline of the slave plantation era were marked not only by the smuggling-in of African slaves but also by the labor-contract importation of many thousands of Yucatecans and Chinese. These semi-free laborers eased the transition from slavery to freedom for the plantation owners by lowering the market price of free labor; thereby they took the burden of the transition upon their own backs. And at the same time that they added to the heterogeneity of Cuban society, they sorely taxed its existing social institutions.

As with the slaves, it was not the physical type of the newcomers but their illiteracy, defenselessness against exploitation, cultural separateness, and degraded social status which made their integration difficult.

But Dr. Guerra may be right in feeling that none of these developments fundamentally altered the character of Cuban society. In the case of the English and the French Antilles, the slave plantation era had utterly erased the European yeoman colonist communities, supplanting these with great masses of African slaves under the control of a few Europeans. In such circumstances, it was almost impossible to create within the islands any cultural continuity, any informed social structure with potentialities for growth and development. Cuba, on the other hand, thanks to the late development of the slave plantation, had had time to create a society with character of its own.

As has been indicated, the slave plantations of the late eighteenth and early nineteenth centuries were larger and more advanced technically than those which preceded them, but they were not immense enterprises. Though operated with slave (and, later, contract) labor, the resident labor force was able to grow much of its food and to fabricate most of its basic domestic requirements. These plantations frequently had resident owners—Frenchmen or Spaniards, but mostly Cubans—and the relationships between the owners (*hacendados*) and the labor force were personal, if not congenial. The hacendados, usually rich and powerful men but not alien to the setting in which they functioned, were the community leaders. They and the men who worked for them as laborers or as slaves, as well as the small-scale cultivators of the countryside, were sometimes aligned politically against Spain and often in agreement on issues dealing with Cuban culture. That is, though the newly developing slave plantations powerfully affected Cuban society, it may be correct to assert that they were unable to change its basic character.

Thus, for instance, much Cuban land remained in subsistence crops and in tobacco, even at the height of slave-plantation expansion. Tobacco, an ideal small-farm crop requiring great personal care and skill to grow properly, was uniquely Cuban; its continuing importance and the contrast it made with sugar—so beautifully analyzed by Dr. Fernando Ortiz in *Cuban Counterpoint*—made clear that the slave plantation had not succeeded in entirely dominating Cuban rural life and values. Cuban novelists, poets, composers, and artists continued to contribute to the mainstream of New World life and letters. The National University remained an important center of learning. The bitter, seemingly endless struggle against Spain, which cruelly lay waste to Cuban lives and land, went on, giving meaning and poignance to *Cubanidad*—"Cuban-ness."

On the eve of the Spanish-American War, Cuba's place in the Antilles spectrum was surely unique. Largest and richest of the islands and European-creole in culture, Cuba exhibited most firmly that quality of ideological and political distinctiveness which is commonly associated with nationhood. Haiti, though sovereign a hundred years, had won its freedom under crushing disadvantages and had changed little from its condition on the eve of independence. The peoples of the British, Dutch, French, and Danish islands were still scarred by their degraded colonial past. Santo Domingo was substantially undeveloped, its society lethargic—resembling Puerto Rico and Cuba at a much earlier time in their histories. In this setting, Cuba was outstanding for its wealth, culture, and promise.

It was in the final two decades of the nineteenth century that the Cuban sugar industry underwent complete technical reorganization. The Ten Years' War, emancipation, the competition from beet sugar on the world market, and market instabilities had forced a consolidation of sugar interests. Significant technical improvements in extraction, and especially the spread of rail service as a means for transporting cane, resulted in a sharp drop in the number of mills operating. By 1894, four years before the Spanish-American War, the nearly 1,500 archaic small mills of the pre-Ten Years' War period had been replaced by 400 relatively modern ones. By 1890, Cuba's famous *central* Constancia was producing 135,000 sacks of sugar per season—the biggest sugar mill in the world. Hence the technical transformation of the Cuban sugar industry had begun long before the island fell under United States political control. But after the Spanish-American War, an entirely new period of growth began; it is with this stage in Cuban history—ca. 1898–1927—that the author of *Sugar and Society* is most concerned.

In Dr. Guerra's view, the political, social, and economic changes which overtook Cuba after 1898 were more penetrating and powerful than anything which had come before. These changes cannot be divorced from United States interests in the Caribbean area. It is important to remember that the technical revolution had come before the United States occupation. In the two decades immediately preceding the occupation, the sugar industry had shaken itself down, so to speak. Small enterprises were replaced by large ones; small mills were eliminated and their surrounding lands pre-empted by large mills. Integrated productive assemblages of mills and land became larger, and the small-scale community nature of the traditional plantations was undermined by the change in scale and in mode of operation. But it was only under the aegis of North American power that the earlier changes were extended throughout the sugar industry and the whole industry vastly enlarged.

The spread of technical advance was accompanied by far-reaching economic changes—in land use and landownership, port development and rail facilities, in quota agreements and tariff legislation—which eventually affected the entire structure of Cuban society. Where the slave plantation system, coming late to maturity, had changed Cuba's character without remaking it, the corporate land-and-factory combine (or *latifundium,* as Dr. Guerra refers to it) went far toward altering Cuba's very identity.[8] North American power and wealth unleashed an enterprise so consuming and insatiable that it bid fair to swallow up the whole of Cuba. The nature of this agricultural juggernaut is described well in a passage from Ortiz' *Cuban Counterpoint:*

The central is now more than a mere plantation; there are no longer any real planters in Cuba. The

8. I have dealt with the parallel transformation in Puerto Rico in "The Culture History of a Puerto Rican Sugar Cane Plantation, 1876–1949," *Hispanic American Historical Review, 33,* May 1953, 224–51. I have tried to describe the effects of this transformation, as seen in the life of one man, in *Worker in the Cane: A Puerto Rican Life History* (New Haven, Yale University Press, 1960).

modern central is not a simple agricultural enterprise, nor even a factory whose production is based on the raw materials on hand. Today it is a complicated "system of land, machinery, transportation, technicians, workers, capital, and people to produce sugar." It is a complete social organism, as live and complex as a city or municipality, or a baronial keep with its surrounding fief of vassals, tenants, and serfs. The latifundium is only the territorial base, the visible expression of this. The central is vertebrated by an economic and legal structure that combines masses of land, masses of machinery, masses of men, and masses of money, all in proportion to the integral scope of the huge organism for sugar production.

Today the sugar latifundium is so constituted that it is not necessary for the tracts of land or farms that constitute it to be contiguous. It is generally made up of a nuclear center around the mill yard, a sort of town, and of outlying lands, adjacent or distant, linked by railroads and under the same general control, all forming a complete empire with subject colonies covered with canefields and forests, with houses and villages. And all this huge feudal territory is practically outside the jurisdiction of public law; the norms of private property hold sway there. The owner's power is as complete over this immense estate as though it were just a small plantation or farm. Everything there is private—ownership, industry, mill, houses, store, police, railroad, port. Until the year 1886 [the final end of slavery in Cuba] the workers, too, were chattels like other property.

The sugar latifundium was the cause of important agro-social developments, such as the monopolizing of land that is not cultivated but lies fallow; the scarcity of garden produce or fruits that would complement the basic crop, which is sugar—the reason for the latifundium's existence—because the effort required for this can be turned to more profitable use from the economic standpoint; the depreciation in value of land that it does not need within the zone monopolized by the central, and so on.

Within the territorial scope of the central, economic liberty suffers serious restrictions. There is not a small holding of land nor a dwelling that does not belong to the owner of the central, nor a fruit orchard or vegetable patch or store or shop that does not form part of the owner's domain. The small Cuban landowner, independent and prosperous, the backbone of a strong rural middle class, is gradually disappearing. The farmer is becoming a member of the proletariat, just another laborer, without roots in the soil, shifted from one district to another. The whole life of the central is permeated by this provisional quality of dependence which is characteristic of colonial populations whose members have lost their stake in their country.[9]

When Dr. Guerra wrote his book in 1927, the expansion of just such monster enterprises had been well underway in Cuba for three decades. It would be gratuitous to repeat here those indices which establish

9. Ortiz, op. cit., pp. 53–54.

fully and unmistakably the role of North American capital and interests in this expansion. The question is not whether North American interests principally developed the Cuban sugar industry after 1900—they did—but, rather, whether this did or did not redound to the benefit of the people of Cuba. The question is a very hard one to answer impartially, since it is quite impossible to know what would have happened had North American capital not flowed so heavily into Cuba. Professor Henry Wallich, writing in 1950, probably gave as reasonable an answer as any to the economic aspect of the question. Sugar, he tells us, accounted for about one-quarter of the Cuban gross national product and gave employment in harvest to perhaps one-third or more of the labor force. This dominance, he shows, had its good side: sugar, more than any other tropical product, benefits from intense application of capital, and heavy capitalization in turn enables cooperant factors (e.g. labor, land) to achieve high levels of productivity, provided that the total supply of these factors is not unlimited.

But sugar had its bad side as well. Professor Wallich indicates that the Cuban economy was, so to speak, lopsided because of sugar. The splitting of the Cuban people into a small, unenterprising group of wealthy landowners and stockholders on the one hand and a large, unskilled, impoverished group of rural wage-earners on the other adversely affected the whole society. Professor Wallich refers to Dr. Guerra's book in describing the tendency of the sugar industry to destroy independent farmers and producers of other crops and to inhibit development of all enterprise past a certain point. (That this tendency never completely fulfilled itself in Cuba, Professor Wallich explains, is because the *relatively* limited labor supply and unfavorable market conditions prevented the sugar industry from running its course.) There was also the problem of what Wallich calls "the sugar mentality"—a kind of economic opportunism or shiftlessness, arising from the awareness that Cuba's economic welfare was at the mercy of persons and forces outside the Cuban setting and operating in what appear to be entirely capricious ways. He writes:

> This tendency to pin all hopes on the international sugar markets gives sugar an economic and political dominance even greater than its true weight in the economy. Sugar dominates the economic policy of the country, and other interest must stand aside in the interest of sugar. This is exemplified, for instance, by Cuban commercial relations with the United States, where *fairly sizable Cuban tariff concessions, limiting the possibilities of domestic industry, have served more or less as the price for a reasonable sugar quota* in the United States market. This tendency of the dominant interest to perpetuate itself leads into a vicious circle that is hard to break. [Italics added.]

In effect, the author is saying here that, in return for its share of the North American consumer market, Cuba repudiated the right to develop industrially. Its tariff concessions to North American exporters left its own industries defenseless.

Finally, Professor Wallich refers to the underemployment of resources—land, labor, and capital—resulting from very heavy emphasis on the production of a single crop. The short harvest season, the concentration of landownership, the discouragement of any sort of diversification or of subsistence cropping, all helped to keep the Cuban economy entangled in a monocrop orientation that systematically underutilized cooperant resources.[10] Bad enough that idle machines must pay interest for an entire year on three to five months' work —but what of men who must eat all year on the same? During the *tiempo muerto* (dead season) in sugar, 20 per cent of Cuba's entire labor force was unemployed; and the dead season lasted from seven to nine months of the year. Professor Wallich has written elsewhere that Cuba "enjoys the dubious distinction of being one of the purest one-crop countries in the Western hemisphere; the problems which are characteristic of most Latin American countries appear in Cuba in their most extreme form."[11]

Part of the North American difficulty in understanding Latin America's rural problems in general, and plantation countries such as Cuba in particular, originates in a semantic confusion. The English word which is used to describe the Latin American countryman is *peasant*. This term was used earlier to label a class of independent small-scale landholders who produce part (at least) of their own subsistence and some item for export to the world market. But in common parlance, this term is much less precise. It generally means no more than a person who somehow makes his living

10. H. C. Wallich, *Monetary Problems of an Export Economy* (Cambridge, Harvard University Press, 1950), pp. 10–12.
11. H. C. Wallich, "Cuba," in S. Harris (ed.), *Economic Problems of Latin America* (New York, McGraw-Hill, 1944), p. 338.

from the soil; who is poor by advanced Western standards; who is illiterate or, at any rate, uneducated; and
who is, in some way or other, oppressed or down-
trodden. One never speaks of a United States farmer as
a peasant, and others would be surprised if one did.
Rarely, the Negro sharecroppers of the American South
will be called a "black peasantry," but the usage sounds
strange to our ears. Europe, Asia, Latin America have
peasants; the United States does not. The connotations
of poverty, illiteracy, and oppression go with the term
in our thinking, and they seem offensive if they are applied to our fellow North Americans. At the same time,
the general meaning which is given to the term enables
its users to lump together the agricultural poor of all
lands in one coarse category.

Such loose usage fails entirely to provide a satisfactory way to describe the rural folk of Latin America.
Even a nodding familiarity with the area reveals that
many social groups, standing in very different relationships to the land, economies, and power systems of
their respective countries could be treated as homo-
geneous by applying the term *peasantry* to them—but
it would be a dangerously spurious homogeneity. And
so it is with the Cuban case. In the countryside of which
Dr. Guerra has written there were to be found relatively prosperous and economically progressive farm
owners or operators, employing labor to plant and cut
their sugar cane and selling it on contract to a neighboring mill. Such men often were literate, sophisticated,
and forward-looking—more like Iowa farmers than
like the stereotype of Latin American "peasants." There
were commercial tobacco growers, some very well off
and others barely subsisting. There were wealthy

ranchers, and there were goatherds; sharecroppers, squatters, and landless wage earners; plantation owners and plantation foremen. All lived from and on the land, but as first defined above, the peasantry constitutes only one sociologically (and economically) specifiable group among them.

Even the most preliminary examination of Cuban rural economic realities compels one to classify separately at least three distinguishable social and economic groups: the small-scale landowners, the leaseholders or sharecroppers, and the landless plantation laborers. While it is true that some men "straddled" these alternate modes of livelihood, most either worked for the plantations or else cultivated their own (or leased or rented or sharecropped) land; such adaptations are sometimes mutually exclusive, or even antagonistic. The peasantry, to specify its sociology, controls the land it works and subsists largely on what it produces. Many rural Cubans were peasants by this definition though more were not.

A very substantial part of the Cuban rural labor force was a proletariat, but a rural proletariat: landless, propertyless, wage-earning, and store-buying.[12] Such people view their lives and their labor differently from peasants; accordingly their values (while they may share a certain "Cuban-ness") differ significantly. For anyone desirous of understanding the rural sector of a Latin American nation, it is a serious error to confuse a peasantry with landless rural wage-earners. Such rural social groupings stand in different relationships to the

12. Cf. S. W. Mintz, "The Folk–Urban Continuum and the Rural Proletarian Community," *American Journal of Sociology, 59,* September 1953, 136–43.

rest of their society and may even be counterposed economically or politically.

Dr. Guerra points out that the plantation (or latifundium) is an urbanizing force. As such it urbanizes
while it proletarianizes. By creating company towns,
by appropriating large areas within which the rural
population must concentrate itself densely, by bringing
improvements in transportation and communication,
by standardizing work practices, by establishing company stores, the latifundium does its powerful best to
create a factory situation, albeit a rural one. And factories in the field are urban in many ways, even though
they are not in cities. A rural proletariat working on
modern plantations inevitably becomes culturally and
behaviorally distinct from the peasantry. Its members
neither have nor (eventually) want land. Their special
economic and social circumstances lead them in another direction. They prefer standardized wage mini-
mums, maximum work weeks, adequate medical and
educational services, increased buying power, and
similar benefits and protections. In these ways, they
differ both from the peasantry—who are often conservative, suspicious, frugal, traditionalistic—and from
the farmers, who are the agricultural businessmen, the
forward-looking, cash-oriented, rural middle class.
Such differentiations do not exhaust the sociology of
the Cuban countryside; but at least they indicate that
to talk of Cuba's "peasantry" as if the rural population were an undifferentiated mass of impoverished
landowners is to miss entirely the complexity of rural
Latin America. Peasants who, by a swift process of
plantation development, have been transformed into
rural proletarians, are no longer the same people.

It was the latifundium which converted Cuba's socially heterogeneous rural areas into plantation complexes. Dr. Guerra shows us how this conversion displaced the independent farmers, weakened the rural middle classes (even while bringing more cash income into the countryside), eliminated subsistence cultivation, created total dependence on cash for its landless employees, and stimulated political consciousness on a class basis. The landless, wage-earning, store-buying, organized countrymen—*not* peasants—who had nothing to sell but their labor (and that little more than five months a year) were perfectly ripened by *latifundismo* for changing their economic perceptions into political action.

When it is noted that, in 1953, there were 489,000 agricultural wage laborers in Cuba and 67,000 unpaid family laborers, a gross indication of the difference between peasantry and proletariat is provided us. Many of the agricultural wage laborers did not work for plantations; but many and probably most of the unpaid family laborers were the wives and children of the traditional, small-scale highland peasantry—*los guajiros* —of Cuba. More than 21 out of every 100 members of the *total* labor force worked in the agricultural phases of sugar production alone and in harvest time the percentage rose; more than 60 out of 100 worked for wages. These data reveal the enormous extent to which Cuba was precisely *not* a peasant country; in fact it was because the peasantry was losing ground to the encroaching latifundium that Dr. Guerra could become so justly concerned for the fate of his country.

But the figures are yet more revealing when combined with those for landownership and control. The 1946 Census indicated that 20 per cent of the farmed area was held by less than one-tenth of one per cent of the farms—that is, one-fifth of all Cuban farmland was divided up among slightly more than 100 farms. Of the total number of farms, 70 per cent were 63 acres or less in area, but accounted for only 11 per cent of the farmland. In other words, the Cuban land situation was archetypal for Latin America: a bimodal distribution, with a few enormous latifundia at one end and many very small farms at the other.

But the dichotomy in Cuba goes farther than this, since the large units were mainly sugar plantations—modern, heavily capitalized, and powerful—and where they spread, the small independent farm disappeared. By and large, the difference between peasantry and proletariat was the difference between highland and plain, between small and large, between other crops and sugar cane, and—some would argue—between white and black. Sugar is a lowland crop, a plantation crop, a colonial crop. Before emancipation as well as after, Cuban plantation owners felt the pinch of labor shortage and filled their needs with outsiders.

The special significance of this process—literally, of converting a nation where land could still be secured by landless free men into one in which this would not be feasible—is not missed by Dr. Guerra. Labor shortage is a relative matter. The importations of African slaves and, later, of contract laborers from Mexico and China were political acts with economic objectives: to secure labor at a lower price and to make it more tractable. After the turn of the century, neither slavery nor contract importations from China and India were

possible. The plantation owners turned instead to the
other Antilles, to the descendants of the slaves in Haiti
and Jamaica. These migrants came to Cuba because
the expanding plantations there gave them greater economic opportunities than they had at home. But of
course they won these expanded economic opportunities at the cost of the landless Cuban rural poor who
had come before them, and the Cuban people were
well aware of it. Between 1912 and 1924, 120,000
Haitians and 110,000 Jamaicans came as contract
laborers to Cuba. Their effect on labor conditions in
Cuba can be readily imagined.

The North American dream, that sons may fulfill
fathers' ambitions, was rarely realized by the children
of the Chinese, Jamaican, or Haitian migrants to Cuba.
Their descendants could not be certain that their integration into Cuban life would be either rapid or successful. The latifundium system was directly responsible
for the heightened importation of migrant workers into
Cuba, as the earlier slave plantation system had been
responsible for the importation of smuggled slaves and
Chinese and Yucatecan contract laborers. These people
were imported for the hardest and poorest-paying labor
of all—cane-cutting—and could rarely find work outside harvest season if they stayed on. Unlike immigrants
to North America, they could not readily become part
of an expanding economy, since the sugar industry
dominated that economy entirely; all they could do was
to force further downward the levels of living of the
Cuban people.

Thus, in the early decades of this century, Dr. Guerra
suggests, Cuba was becoming a country in which the
best land was owned on a large scale and by foreigners,

and worked by foreigners as well. His words in this connection ring strangely:

> A country which is politically unfree, but which possesses and cultivates its own lands, can win its freedom, as Cuba did. But a free people who relinquish their land to another have taken the path to economic servitude and social and political decay. . . . Within a quarter of a century, either the latifundium or the republic will no longer exist. The Cuban people will have land and independence, or they will have lost them both. That, not annexation, is Cuba's manifest destiny in the twentieth century.

Perhaps some perspective on the Cuban situation of which Dr. Guerra writes can come from imagining the United States as the agricultural country it was in, say, 1860. Let us imagine further that half of all its farmland is given over to the sugar beet, and up to a third of its entire labor force is engaged in sugar-beet cultivation. The transformation of one important crop into practically the nation's only product would have been accomplished in about thirty years; at the end of that thirty years, one-fifth of the farmland would be engrossed by one-tenth of one per cent of all the farms; and nine of the ten largest estates would be owned by foreigners. The number of small-scale independent landowners would have decreased sharply, and immense immigrations of foreigners—on a scale to dwarf the entries in the early years of this century—would push down the market value of labor. The one-third of the labor force engaged in beet-sugar production would be fully employed a maximum of five months out of the year.

But most importantly, those who live from the yield of this production would be quite unable to diversify the economy in any way or to utilize effectively idle available resources in the slack season. In fact, in order to keep the one good market in which beet sugar is sold, the United States would in effect have to make tariff concessions to the powerful industrial nation which promoted United States agriculture and sold it finished goods, thereby limiting its industrial growth as well as its agricultural diversification. If we are capable seriously of conceiving what these circumstances would do to the (North) American way of life, then we can begin to understand the concern Dr. Guerra felt when he wrote *Sugar and Society.*

And yet Dr. Guerra makes very clear that his hostility is not directed against the sugar industry or foreign capital, but—in his own words—against a system of land exploitation. The fact is that Dr. Guerra is much more moderate than many Cuban critics.[13] In the later editions of *Sugar and Society,* in the prefaces and in footnotes (some of which are omitted here), and in his book *La Industria Azucarera de Cuba* (1940), he points to concrete improvements, such as the development of more equitable factory-farmer contracts, the stoppage of mass labor immigration, and the like. One can only be impressed by the author's care and sense of fairness.

In the light of other data, however, it is difficult not

13. See, for instance, H. Portell Vilá, "La Industria Azucarera y Su Futuro," *Revista Bimestre Cubana, 50,* September–October 1942, pp. 161–79.

to be disturbed by Cuba's economic situation in the years between the publication of the third edition of Dr. Guerra's book and the fall of the Batista government. Wallich's careful observations[14] indicate that the Cuban sugar industry of the 1940s still was not adequately serving the interests of the Cuban people. "Dead time" still left human and machine resources idle and people hungry. The International Bank report for 1950 urgently but vainly called attention to the paralyzing dominance of the sugar industry, while the Batista regime's ambitious development plan (1954–58) artificially held up per capita income but, according to one author,[15] "did not improve the productive capacity and had little effect on the chronic unemployment. . . . The average income figures were largely meaningless, however, as they included a small number of great fortunes on the one hand and widespread poverty on the other."

Social and health data are no more comforting. According to MacGaffey and Barnett,[16] in 1953 2.3 per cent of rural Cuban homes had inside piped water, while 85 per cent were supplied by rivers and springs; 3 per cent had modern toilets, while 54 per cent had no sanitary facilities of any kind. Rural illiteracy in Oriente province reached 50 per cent in 1953, while the figure for rural Cuba as a whole in that year was 42 per cent. The 1950 Mission of the International Bank for Reconstruction and Development reported that 60 per cent of rural Cubans had serious nutritional

14. H. Wallich, op. cit., 1944, 1950. See also the appendix to this edition by Dr. Guerra's son, José Guerra y Debén.

15. W. MacGaffey and C. R. Barnett, *Cuba* (New Haven, HRAF Press, 1962), p. 60.

16. Ibid., pp. 41, 164–66.

deficiencies, while 80–90 per cent of rural children were infested with intestinal parasites. Improved or not, the sugar industry was not kind enough to Cubans.

Eric Williams, one of the most eloquent historians of the Caribbean, has written: "Strange that an article like sugar, so sweet and necessary to human existence, should have occasioned such crimes and bloodshed!"[17] Strange, indeed; and stranger yet, perhaps, that the history of sugar is a record of so many unheeded warnings. One cannot read in that history without wondering at the recklessness of men, as well as at their greed and cruelty. Sugar still rules the Antilles. In the old areas of settlement, cane grows in fields where it was planted one, two, three, or four centuries ago; in some of these same fields, it is possible to turn up shards which remain from the aboriginal dwellers of the islands. History has written very heavily in these islands. But the Antilles have a future as well as a past. To suppose that the problems of which Dr. Guerra has written with such cogency and feeling are now entirely solved would be unhappily naïve. In much of the Caribbean area the chronic unemployment, malnutrition, inadequate social services, and heedless but massive foreign influence still keep plantation populations deprived and politically labile. It cannot be supposed that the disturbances of recent years are now at an end. Don Ramiro Guerra wrote in 1927 hoping to help make the future a good one; what he wrote then is still worth reading.

17. In *Capitalism and Slavery* (Chapel Hill, University of North Carolina Press, 1944), p. 27.

Introduction

Latifundia perdidere other countries besides
Italy.—*H. E. Egerton, Professor of Colonial
History, University of Oxford, in Foreword
to* History of Barbados, *p. viii.*[1]

In the introduction to the first volume of *Historia de
Cuba,* we commented on the fact, already noted by
earlier writers,[2] that all of the Caribbean islands which

1. V. T. Harlow, *History of Barbados, 1624–1685* (Oxford,
Clarendon Press, 1926).

2. It has been pointed out that the great Cuban writer, José
Antonio Saco, dealt with this question in several of his works, and
I am pleased to acknowledge this. See Raúl Lorenzo, *Sentido Na-
cionalista del Pensamiento de Saco* (Havana, 1942). [Note to the
third edition.]

remained under Spanish rule until the nineteenth century were predominantly white communities, whereas the colonies of other European nations were almost exclusively Negro communities. This held true even for Haiti and Jamaica, which were originally settled by whites, but were later dominated by the colored population, after being taken over by France and England respectively. On the one hand Cuba, with slightly more than 3,500,000 inhabitants,[3] has a colored population which makes up 28 per cent of the total; Puerto Rico, with approximately 1,400,000 inhabitants, has an even smaller proportion of Negroes; and a high proportion of the Dominican Republic's 900,000 inhabitants are white. On the other hand, Barbados, a British possession in the Lesser Antilles, is inhabited by 15,000 whites and 180,000 Negroes; Jamaica, also British, has 14,476 and 817,643 respectively; and Haiti has 2,045,000 inhabitants, all of whom are colored. If we examine the population composition of the other Antilles, and even of the countries on the Caribbean coasts of Central and South America, we find the same situation: every portion of the area occupied and settled by the French, Dutch, and English, some parts as early as the seventeenth century, has become a plantation colony with a very small proportion of white inhabitants. Of all the colonies established on the coasts of the Caribbean, the only ones well organized socially and economically and destined to become independent, progressive nations seem to have been founded by Spain.

3. The population figures given for Cuba and the other Antillean islands are those of 1925. [Note to the third edition.]

At first glance, we were reluctant to assert the superiority of Spanish colonizing methods over those of the Dutch, French, and English, and were strongly disposed to attribute this curious fact to the influence of the climate, which was more easily tolerated by the Spaniards than by the rest of the Europeans. In the *Historia de Cuba* referred to earlier, we remarked on the Spaniard's greater resistance to the rigors of a tropical climate, as compared with the English, Dutch, and French. But though we thought it might have been an important factor, we never claimed that climate was the exclusive cause of this significant demographic difference. For one thing, the Spaniards, who were the first colonizers and settlers of Haiti and Jamaica, were themselves supplanted in those countries by colored populations. Feeling sure that there must be some extremely powerful but obscure forces at work, we continued methodically to investigate this fundamentally important phenomenon. Now we are convinced that we have solved what might be called the mystery of the substitution of a Negro population for a white population in the Antilles. In addition, we have been able to draw the following conclusions, which we consider to be of great significance for the present and future of Cuba.

First, the sugar latifundium is responsible for the substitution of one population for another. Second, the process of substitution has always developed according to a set cycle which must be preceded by a transfer of property ownership. This cycle began its powerful course in Cuba in this century, which means that the menace is a present-day threat and did not originate in the colonial period. Therefore, the evil that confronts us is not really colonial, but has been brought about by economic and financial forces as likely to operate in a free and sovereign nation as in a colony. Third, the racial question is entirely secondary to the creation of a social and economic organization based on exploiters and exploited. The Africans and their Antillean descendants, socially more defenseless than the whites, were more easily subjugated by the economic pressures of the latifundium and were reduced to actual slavery in the past and to economic servitude in the present. We are not, however, dealing with a question of race but with a system of land exploitation that divides the population into two groups: a small number of capitalist agents who direct and administer sugar cane planting and sugar manufacture and shipping, and a mass of laborers of whatever race obliged to accept a minimal wage and to tolerate a reduced standard of living, according to the circumstances of each place—Negroes in Jamaica and Barbados, Negroes and Indians in Trinidad and British Guiana, Negroes and whites in Cuba and Puerto Rico, and so on.

It has often been said that history is of no practical value for the study of contemporary social problems, that it consists of no more than names and dates together with vague and debatable moralizing. We do not deny that this is true of the sort of so-called history which treats only of heroes and battles. But there is another kind of history that, although less luminous, spectacular, and exciting, is dedicated to elucidating the factors that have determined and still determine the development of communities and peoples. This history explains certain facts of economics that previously seemed due to chance or to the mysterious play of hidden forces beyond man's control. It furnishes man with information which enables him to intervene by choice, with knowledge and foresight, in the course of events that may reshape societies and alter their destinies.

Each of the many Antillean islands has developed separately and so has constituted a microcosm, a limited arena for historical observation and research. Certain constants of social change, such as the land tenure system and the sugar latifundium, have operated independently in each of the islands and, under similar circumstances, have always produced an identical cycle of events. In this volume we have tried to trace the development of the sugar latifundium in the Antilles as it effects the transformation of a social group;[4] and the facts of these changes have led us to express certain conclusions.

At this time Cuba is faced with many serious problems related to landownership, the rapid disappearance of independent rural proprietors, and the crushing advance of the latifundium. The future depends on how satisfactorily it resolves those problems.

These chapters will support the statement quoted from Egerton, that *latifundia perdidere* other countries besides the Italy of antiquity. If our government, our legislators, and Cuban public opinion are made

---

4. For our discussion of the British West Indies we have drawn largely upon the distinguished work of a select group of English historians: L. M. Penson, *The Colonial Agents of the British West Indies* (London, 1924); C. S. S. Higham, *The Development of the Leeward Islands under the Restoration* (Cambridge, 1921); J. A. Williamson, *The Caribbee Islands under the Proprietary Patents* (Oxford, 1926); V. T. Harlow, *Colonising Expeditions of the West Indies and Guiana, 1623–1667* (London, Hakluyt Society, 1925) and *History of Barbados, 1624–1685;* W. Law Mathieson, *British Slavery and Its Abolition, 1823–1838* (London, 1926).

aware of the dangers implicit in the economic and social change now taking place in Cuba, a change which could ruin us and drag us down socially and politically, we shall be satisfied that we have fulfilled one of our duties as a Cuban and as a historian.

Part One

The Destructive Effect
of the Large Sugar Plantation
in the British West Indies

1 The Case of Barbados

> In the early years sugar had brought great wealth to the island, but already it was beginning to effect that social and economic decay which is so striking a feature of West Indian history.—*Harlow,* History of Barbados, *p. 265.*

The island of Barbados, easternmost of the Lesser Antilles, has a very small area—some 166 square miles—and a population of 195,000 inhabitants, of whom 15,000 are white and 180,000 are colored. Because of its limited territory, Barbados offers exceptionally favorable conditions for the study of the characteristic evolution of the large sugar plantation, which here completed its social and economic transformation with great rapidity. Barbados, as Egerton has said,[1] is a

1. *History of Barbados,* p. vii.

remarkable microcosm, whose history presents to us in miniature, and in the space of a few years, the same process that has taken place and continues to take place in the other sugar-producing islands of the Antilles over periods of time directly in proportion to the size of each. In Cuba, the largest of the islands, occupation of all the territory by the sugar latifundium will take longer, but the invasion of thousands of *caballerías* (a *caballería* equals 33.16 acres) over the last fifteen years makes it clear that, if it continues to advance at the same speed and unless it is restrained by adequate measures or by accidental circumstances, it will inevitably dominate more than four-fifths of the country.

The history of Barbados may be summarized in a few lines. In 1625 an English mariner, John Powell, returning to his country from Pernambuco, landed on Barbados and, finding it uninhabited, took possession of the island in the name of England. Two years later colonization was begun by a commercial company under the direction of Sir William Courteen. Its activities met with difficulties because a grant of all the Caribbean islands, including Barbados, had been obtained from King James I by the Earl of Carlisle, a favorite at the English court. Courteen sought the support of another influential courtier, the Earl of Pembroke, who in turn secured a patent. There followed a series of quarrels in England and struggles on the island between the Courteen and Carlisle factions, which retarded the development of Barbados. Nevertheless, the population increased rapidly. In 1628 Barbados had 1,400 inhabitants, all settlers from England; in 1636 it had 6,000; and in 1643 there were 37,000 inhabitants of English origin, the highest number in the island's history. Its principal products in those early years were tobacco, cotton, indigo, pepper, citrus fruits, cattle and pigs, poultry, and other consumer goods. Production of sugar did not begin until after 1640.

A large proportion of the population was made up of planters who obtained their estates from the Lord Proprietor; many of them belonged to the nobility who had fled or were exiled from England during the upheavals and civil wars of that epoch. The majority of the population consisted of indentured servants who contracted in England to work for their masters for a given period of years, usually four. These indentured servants, who existed in all the English colonies of the Antilles, found on arrival in the island that they were reduced to actual slavery. As in the case of the *indios encomendados* (enfeoffed Indian workers) of Cuba, they were treated worse than slaves because they could not count even on the protection afforded the slave by his owner's self-interest. Sometimes they plotted rebellions in the islands, and when the Spanish squadron under Don Fadrique de Toledo attacked the English occupying St. Kitts (September 1630), the indentured servants there rose against their masters and aided Don Fadrique. Enslaved by their own countrymen, they sided in despair with their traditional enemy—the Spanish—for the sake of recovering their freedom. However, these bondsmen enjoyed one advantage, and this was the main incentive to their signing the indenture articles: when the contract expired they were given a piece of land, which made them small property owners and independent farmers. In this way, small holdings multiplied in Barbados, and fifteen years after it was founded it was one of the most prosperous and populous of the English colonies, with sufficient resources to resist any attack by the Spanish.

The cultivation of sugar cane rapidly changed this situation, so rich in reality and in promise. Harlow says that the first person in Barbados to plant his land with sugar cane was probably Colonel Holdip, toward the beginning of the fifth decade (1640). Other farmers hastened to follow his example and they sent to Brazil, then in the hands of the Dutch, for sugar cane cuttings, farm equipment, and general instructions. Their first efforts were discouraging because they had not fully understood the methods of sugar production; for two or three years their sugar was meager and of little commercial value. But the more enterprising planters had the good sense to visit Brazil themselves where long experience had revealed the best techniques. There they learned to correct their mistakes, not only in cultivating the cane but in its harvest and manufacture, and the sugar industry improved.

By 1647 many sugar mills had already been set up. Nonetheless, the sugars they produced were only *muscovados,* which contained so much syrup and so many impurities that they were hardly worth sending to England, where they could be sold only with difficulty. But by 1650 considerable experience had been gained and increasing quantities of sugar were being shipped to European markets. As a result, the island developed amazingly between 1640 and 1650, though England's trade and industry in the same period remained stationary. In 1666 experts estimated that, since beginning to produce sugar, Barbados had increased its wealth seventeenfold. A contemporary historian points out that a plantation valued at £400 before changing over to sugar was sold in 1648 for £14,000.

This was an extraordinary period of "fat years," when fortunes were made overnight. Later, when production almost equaled demand and competition became keener, the plantation owners learned to be satisfied with a quarter of their original profits.

The sudden expansion of an island of scanty resources into one of the wealthiest of the English plantation colonies of the New World during an epoch when the mother country found itself submerged in the horrors of civil war was made possible, says Harlow, by the wide use of Dutch capital. Dutch bankers and merchants extended credit against the first crop for farming equipment and material to construct sugar mills, as well as for Negro slaves, who were being provided in great numbers to the principal estates. The Dutch willingly postponed collecting these debts until the cane was planted, harvested, and made into sugar. Contemporary historians say that without the stimulus of foreign capital the island would never have been able to develop so important an industry in so short a time.

But curiously enough, adds Harlow, this swiftly achieved and economically beneficial prosperity eventually proved to be the main cause of the island's decline. When Barbados still produced a variety of crops, the land was divided into small holdings occupied by numerous small proprietors. This system, found in the majority of new colonies, was partly the result of the distribution of small farms to the first settlers. It also resulted from the custom of granting to each white servant ten or twenty acres of land when his indenture ended. As a consequence, the island was dominated by a prosperous farming class which filled the militia and was the backbone of the colony.

With the coming of the sugar industry this healthy situation changed. In order to be run economically, a sugar plantation needed extensive acreage and an abundance of cheap labor. The long-term credit system of the Dutch provided for both requirements, but only to the wealthy planters who could offer solid guarantees; the small farmer with limited holdings and little capital could not meet the considerable initial expense of establishing a sugar mill. The land, therefore, fell more and more into the hands of a "coterie of magnates," says Harlow, and their land purchases resulted in a surprising reduction in the number of inhabitants. Emigrating at the first opportunity, the dispossessed represented an irreparable loss to the colony. An example of this process may be found in the property of Captain Watermann, which covered 800 acres and which, before the sugar fever, had been occupied by forty families of small landholders.

African slave labor, much cheaper than white European labor, increased with great rapidity. The slave population, a source of anxiety and weakness in all the colonies where it had been introduced, amounted to 5,680 in 1645, and had risen to 82,023 by 1667. The history of Barbados is based on this twofold process by which a sturdy English colony was converted into little more than a sugar factory, owned by a few capitalists living abroad and worked by a mass of alien laborers.

By 1685 the process was finished. Since that date the history of Barbados has been uneventful. The descendants of the slaves are legally free but, with daily wages averaging only 25 cents, they live in misery.

2 Slaves Versus Free Farmers

> For the money which procured a white man's service for ten years could buy a negro for life.—*Harlow,* History of Barbados, *p. 307.*

The case of Barbados illustrates a fundamental of Antillean history: the substitution of cheap slave labor for the small-scale landholder. This was not the inevitable result of race or climate and beyond human control—a theory accepted by the slave owners of yesterday, and still maintained by the plantation owners of today. Its cause was purely social and economic: the destruction of the small holding by the sugar latifundium and the consequent emigration of an active, enterprising social class which left voluntarily in order to escape the hunger and the lower standard of living brought about by lack of work. Actually, it was not the Antillean climate that drove out the whites, but the capitalist sugar industry which, in its search for unlimited profits, did away with the small holding and changed young, robust, self-sustaining communities into mere workshops, where low-priced labor was exploited for the exclusive benefit of distant commercial and banking centers.

Emigration became intense between 1650 and 1660. Authorities and early settlers of Barbados were well aware of the true cause of this exodus: the monopolization of the land, which made it impossible to continue the practice of distributing lots to white bondsmen on the termination of their contracts, and the large-scale purchase of sugar cane from small property holders by the wealthiest sugar manufacturers. In 1647, the Earl of Carlisle, as Lord Proprietor, was forced to post notice that there was no more land available for bondsmen who had completed their contracts and that it could be supplied to them only in neighboring islands such as Nevis and Antigua. Emigration to these islands and to Jamaica and British Guiana, all with the same climate as Barbados, is ample proof that economic and social conditions, and not climate, were the principal factors involved.

The governor of Barbados, Francis Lord Willoughby, realizing that the departure of its white settlers would ruin the island and would promote rival colonies and threaten its security, tried to restrain the emigrants from going beyond the nearest islands in their search for land, and he even occupied by force the French island of St. Lucia. But all his efforts proved useless because the latifundium continued to expel the small farmers, who fled to Jamaica (occupied by England in

1655), St. Kitts, Tobago, Nevis, Trinidad, British
Guiana, and even to Virginia in North America. Harlow
says:[1]

> The concentration of land in Barbados in the
> hands of a comparatively small body of great land-
> owners was driving the poorer class of white men
> to seek land in other settlements. The movement
> contributed to a marked expansion of colonial
> empire, but gradually reduced Barbados from the
> position of a populous virile colony to that of a
> politically unimportant sugar plantation, owned
> by absentee proprietors and worked by negro
> slaves. . . . In the early years sugar had brought
> great wealth to the island, but already it was be-
> ginning to effect that social and economic decay
> which is so striking a feature of West Indian
> history.

The white population (37,200 in 1634), uprooted
from the soil by the latifundium system, began to decrease in 1645. By 1653 it had been reduced to 30,000
inhabitants; by 1668 to 20,000; by 1786 to 16,167,
where it remained for more than a century; and by 1922
there were no more than 15,000 white inhabitants. The
climatic explanation can be eliminated simply by ob-
serving where the emigrants chose to re-establish themselves. Harlow quotes[2] an author who in 1667 drew
the following picture of emigration from Barbados:

> At least 12,000 former landholders and trades-
> men have gone off, "wormed out of their small

1. *History of Barbados,* pp. 153, 265.
2. Ibid., p. 340.

settlements by theire more suttle and greedy neigh-
bours. . . . Between 1643 and 1647 to New England, 1,200; to Trinidad and Tobago, 600; between 1646 and 1658 to Guadaloupe, Martinique,
Marie-galante, Granada, Tobago, and Curazao,
1,600; with Colonel Venables to Hispaniola and
since to Jamaica, 3,300." More than 5,000 left
Barbados on the various expeditions to the Leeward Islands during the wars with the French and
Dutch, very few of whom ever returned. After
1667 the exodus of time-expired servants and
others to Carolina and elsewhere consistently outnumbered the arrivals in Barbados from the
Mother Country. In 1670 no less than 2,000 colonists left Barbados for other plantations.

Parallel to the decrease in the white society of small
property owners was the rapid and constant increase
in the slave population. In 1636 there was no record of
African slaves in Barbados. In 1643, three years after
the introduction of the sugar industry, there were already 6,000; in 1655 there were 20,000; by 1668 the
number of slaves had increased to 40,000 and was
double that of the white population; in 1792 it amounted to 64,330; and in 1835, when slavery was finally
abolished, 82,000. One might wonder why the small
landholders could not have remained on the island as a
salaried working class. But the same economic factor
that uprooted them from the soil prevented them from
finding work. Says Harlow:[3]

Cultivation of large plantations necessitated the
use of manual labour on a large scale. Soon plant-

3. Ibid., p. 307.

ers discovered that . . . the money which procured a white man's service for ten years could buy a negro for life.

From the moment the Dutch slave trader agreed to accept sugar in payment for his wares, the fate of the free white laborer was decided. At first he was still used in work that required certain manual abilities or technical skills. But as soon as the slaves became trained in all the trades, the white day laborer's only recourse was emigration. It was not a question of Negro and white, of European and African, but of underpaid as opposed to expensive labor. The problem was not racial, but social and economic.

As we shall see, the abolition of slavery did not redeem the colored man from his economic servitude in Barbados or in any of the other small islands. Since by that time the last inch of land was in the hands of the latifundia, the day he became free he found himself faced with a terrible dilemma, basically the same as that which had earlier confronted the white settlers: whether to emigrate or to work for the minimal daily wage imposed by the plantation owners. Emigrate? Where to? Neither the poor freedmen nor their descendants, less fortunate than the white farmers of the first epoch, have been able to escape the iron economic yoke of the latifundium. Harlow in 1926 writes:[4]

> Modern visitors to Barbados report the existence of widespread bitterness against the white man. The black labourer, whose wage is only a shilling a day, finds it hard in these days of high prices to avoid starvation, and nurses resentment accord-

4. Ibid., p. 329.

ingly. On the other hand, the planter maintains, and with much truth, that the average negro labourer does so little for his money that a higher wage would be an economic impossibility.

It is evident that in the third decade of the twentieth century, just as in the seventeenth century, the sugar planter in Barbados continues to work for the fortune and welfare of the few at the expense of the poverty and suffering of the masses. In place of independent agriculture, he has undertaken to bring about the economic servitude of Negro and white.

3 Land and Labor
Under the Latifundium System

Unfortunately the name of freedom was pros-
tituted by planters whose only aim was self-
aggrandisement.—*Harlow,* History of Barbados, *p. 127.*

Forced labor was replaced [in the West
Indies] by labor which although voluntary
was poorly paid; the African violently
wrenched from his land was succeeded by
the Asian tricked into a contract and incorporated into the rural masses of America.
—*Report of the Cuban Commissioners to
the Information Board in 1866; Proposal on
Immigration made by the Count of Pozos
Dulces.*

As Harlow says, the history of the British West Indies is fundamentally one of social and political decay. The history of Barbados was repeated in the other islands, including Jamaica, the largest one, occupied in 1655 by Penn and Venables, to whom Cromwell had assigned the ambitious task of expelling the Spaniards from America. The farmers of Barbados helped colonize other settlements, which went through the same cycle: the conveyance of the land to the wealthiest sugar planters (for the most part absentee); the disappearance of small and medium-sized properties; the emigration of the white farmer; the wholesale importation of slaves. Only the farmer who went to Virginia or New England fared better, because there he had unlimited available land on which to found a permanent home.

By the end of the seventeenth century Barbados had lost the political importance of its early years, and this was also true of the other British colonies in the West Indies. Reduced to the lowly position of plantation colonies, they presented the same monotonous and dismal historical panorama: hundreds of thousands of unhappy slaves, working and dying under the cruelest oppression, so that sugar could be provided as cheaply as possible to the great London market. The social and economic organization hardened into a definite, immutable form: the latifundium planter above and the African slave below.

Within this society, so rudimentary in form, there was no social force which could bring about change, progress, or any improvement. It was not conceivable that the owner of a sugar estate, generally a rich merchant in the city or a lord with a seat in Parliament, would voluntarily surrender any part of his profits or his properties for the benefit of some miserable slaves, a thousand leagues distant, crushed by their labor and degraded by their servitude. Nor is it possible to imagine any way by which these poor wretches could have communicated with each other, organized, and devised some means to shake off the yoke. The white population was limited in each island to the strict minimum needed to administer the plantations, govern the colony, collect the taxes, and control the slaves; it did not increase because the island offered no incentive of any kind to attract new settlers from Europe. Since the existing situation could neither worsen nor improve, in generation after generation the same exploitation, suffering, and misery were repeated.

In 1833 an apparently fundamental change of a social and political nature took place: the English Parliament approved the law abolishing slavery and re-established as a preliminary measure what Mathieson[1] refers to as the apprenticeship system. The law provided that only those under six years of age would be immediately freed and that all others would have to continue as apprentices with their masters for six more years, binding themselves to work without salary seven and a half hours a day in return for food, clothing, and lodging. If we estimate ten hours to a workday, the slave could, under the law, work for himself during one quarter of the day, or two and a half hours. The law also provided that, to compensate owners for this reduction of two and a half hours, the British government would allocate twenty million pounds for distri-

1. W. L. Mathieson, *British Slave Emancipation, 1838–1849* (London, Longmans, Green, 1932).

bution among the sugar planters. The slave could use his two and a half free hours to work where he pleased, but the planters were obliged to offer him employment at a fixed salary in proportion to the price he would bring on the market. The salary was to be equal, each year, to one-sixth of the slave's market price and was to be credited to his account, so that at the end of a six-year apprenticeship he could purchase his freedom. Owners, if they so wished, were authorized to free their slaves immediately.

The execution of this law demonstrated a basic economic, social, and political fact: the completely free colored man without land to work as an independent farmer would continue to be as oppressed and exploited as before.

The first example of this, a typical one, occurred on the island of Antigua. Its Legislative Assembly, composed of planters, agreed in 1834 "to relieve the slave population of all the duties imposed upon it by the recent law of Parliament," and declared slavery to be totally abolished. After this apparently generous measure was approved by the Colonial Secretary, it went into effect on August 1 of that year. Mathieson relates that Negroes and whites gathered together in all the churches to give thanks for the happy conclusion of slavery on the island, and it was a noble spectacle to see masters attending religious services with slaves, clasping their hands affectionately and sharing their joy. Saturday was also a holiday and the following Monday, on beginning their free lives, His Britannic Majesty's new subjects learned that the planters had agreed with one another to fix a salary for all the island of one shilling for the most skilled workers and nine pennies for the rest. This wretched wage was less expensive to the planters than the maintenance, clothing, and lodging of each slave. The planters gained from the emancipation above and beyond the indemnity they received from their motherland.

It was a cruel joke on the Negroes and on the generosity of Parliament. The latifundium owners could carry out this plan, wrote Governor Lord Sligo, because Antigua is an island where the last acre of land was in the hands of the planters and where most of the provisions were imported; therefore, in order to buy each day's food in the market with their daily wages, the Negroes had no recourse but to work under the conditions set for them. The cost of sugar production did not increase, the planters earned higher profits, and Lord Brougham could tell Parliament that England had received nothing in exchange for the twenty million pounds sterling it had given to the owners of West Indian slaves.

The situation in Antigua was repeated except for details in all the little islands of the British West Indies. The freedmen could not emigrate with their families because they had no resources and no place to go. They submitted then, and continue to do so, and they offer one more terrible proof to the world that social and political liberty, without economic liberty, is a shadow, a fiction, a myth. For the farmer the essence of economic liberty is his possession of a piece of land where he can raise his crops and live.

Jamaica, Trinidad, and British Guiana differed in that not all their lands were occupied or entirely owned by the planters. Knowing that they would not be able to impose low wages on liberated Negroes, the lati-

fundium owners mustered all their forces to oppose
abolition. The apprenticeship system, therefore, lasted
in Jamaica until 1838; meanwhile the planters, since
they did not own all the arable land, exhausted every
possible means to ensure a minimal wage scale for the
freedmen.

Mathieson[2] cites in this connection a measure proposed by the planters which has perhaps no equal in
history as evidence of the extremes to which human
self-interest will go: a heavy tax would be laid on all
lands to be used for crops so that the Negroes would
have no way to nourish themselves and would be compelled to accept whatever daily wage was set for them.
Another procedure used was to charge a high rent on
the thatched huts that the freedmen had built for themselves on the plantations, forcing them almost overnight to give up everything they owned and move great
distances to unpopulated regions without shelter of any
kind. The planters, says Mathieson, knowing how attached the Africans were to their little plots of subsistence land, each with its own familial burying ground,
hoped that the prospect of abandoning these would
bring about their capitulation.

Helped by some missionaries, the freedmen, who
showed extraordinary patience and restraint, protected
themselves to the best of their abilities. Under the direction of Pastor Knibb and financed by money sent by
English abolitionist societies, they acquired enough
property to found the settlement of Birmingham, with
adjacent farmland, which served as a model for almost
two hundred similar Negro colonies created over the

2. Ibid., p. 61.

next four years. Thanks to the availability of farmland, the colored workers were able to defend themselves, and their firm stand resulted in a higher wage scale and much more favorable conditions in Jamaica than in the smaller islands. In some regions they were able to develop a diversified agriculture which still exists today.

But the plantation system, which turns agriculture into a business, requires cheap labor above all. In colonies where the planters did not control all the land, they could not force down wages as had been done in Antigua, and they turned to the method now employed in Cuba—the importation of low-cost laborers to compete with the native worker who tills his own soil.

British India has been in recent years the principal source of contracted cheap labor, just as in Barbados in the seventeenth century it was the English indentured servant and in Cuba in the middle of the last century it was the Chinese. In Cuba today the Haitians are imported for cheap labor. Few of us know that of the 304,412 inhabitants of British Guiana in 1925, more than 125,000 were East Indians; that in Trinidad there are 120,000 East Indians; and that even in Jamaica, at our doorstep, there are more than 18,000. The latifundium owner continues his exploitation in the Antilles, imposing his will where he owns all the land, as in Antigua and other small islands, or importing cheap labor to keep down the wages of the native workers where the latter can still dig in and defend themselves. Now he threatens to extend the same social, economic, and political decadence to other Caribbean countries, including more fortunate islands like Cuba which, for reasons to be discussed, were safe from his oppressive grip until the end of the last century.

Part Two

The Historical Process
of the Appropriation and Division
of Land in Cuba

4 Two Contrasting Destinies

> A country's agriculture is not the result of caprice or prejudice. It rests on the society which produced it, and it develops according to the institutions which govern that society. It will grow and flourish, or stagnate and decay, together with those institutions. The agricultural process is intimately related to the other institutional forces which give shape to the character and government of a people.—*Report of the Cuban Commissioners to the Information Board in 1866.*

When Spain occupied Cuba in the second decade of the sixteenth century, all the land, under traditional Castilian law, was considered *realenga*—that is, the property of the King in his role of *Dominus rerum,* master of all things. During that long period in which Catholic Spain was destroying the Moslem occupation, the Castilian kings had regarded the land they recovered from the Moors as realenga and had redistributed it among their needy subjects. They were then able to create along the Arab frontier a series of strong settlements fiercely defended by Christians who were determined not to surrender one inch of their newly acquired property. This practice, continued over the centuries, so effectively extended Castilian influence into southern Spain that conquest and settlement became inseparable in the minds of the monarchs.

The Catholic kings, whose glory was the reconquest of all Spanish soil, applied the same system to the Indies. On June 18, 1513, two years after the occupation of Cuba had begun, King Ferdinand issued in Valladolid a royal decree:

> so that our subjects may be encouraged to go forth to settle in the Indies and so that they may live with all the comfort that we wish for them, it is our will that there be distributed houses, lots, and lands to all those who go to colonize new regions in those places . . . and having labored and built dwellings on those lands and having resided four years in those places, we grant them the right from that moment on to sell and to do with that property as they please, freely and independently.

Don Diego de Velázquez, the first Cuban governor, was charged with carrying out the royal decree to distribute realenga lands among the original Spanish colonizers of the island. Therefore, the first division and allotments of Cuban land were guided by a purpose radically different from that of the English kings a century later when they disposed of Barbados and the other Caribbean islands occupied by Great Britain. The English practice was designed to enrich an influential individual; the Spanish, to promote their colonization of the Indies. This initial difference between Castilian and English policies in the Caribbean eventually had incalculable consequences.

Velázquez distributed little land, owing to the limited number of settlers. The discovery and conquest of the wealthy Aztec and Inca empires had drawn off most Spanish immigrants to the continent, and the bulk of Cuban territory remained unoccupied as realenga land. There is no evidence that the governors who succeeded Velázquez after his death in 1524 made any new allotments.

In 1536 the *Cabildo* (municipal corporation) of Sancti Spiritus, although it had no legal power to do so, yielded to the petition of one Fernando Gómez and, "considering it a service to His Majesty and of benefit to the township that the savannas should be stocked with cattle," granted him a range of three leagues known by the name of Manicaragua, and so created the first cattle latifundium. The Cabildo used the phrase "without prejudice to a third party" in order to free itself of all responsibility, but it may have felt justified in acting in the name of the King because of the almost complete isolation of the town governments of that period and because the staffs carried by the councilmen were customarily referred to as "for the King." This daring decision of the Council of Sancti Spiritus created a legal precedent for other cabildos on the island, especially those of Havana and Sancti Spiritus itself, for continuing to make land grants in the same manner. The procedure could not have been more democratic and the land could not have gone to any group with more legitimate claim than the long-time residents of the region.

The Crown, having almost abandoned the administration of Cuba as an entirely unproductive island, sent to Havana in 1574 the magistrate of the *Audiencia* (royal court of appeal) of Santo Domingo, which had jurisdiction over the country. Alonso Cáceres, who was charged with conducting the *residencia* (judicial review) of the governor and putting in order the affairs of the councils, was a conscientious and hard-working magistrate. After thoroughly investigating the situation on the island, he drafted and put into effect many excellent government measures, among which were the Municipal Ordinances that bear his name. Although these were not approved by the King until much later, they comprised a very broad body of law, extraordinary for the period, full of wisdom and common sense. Accepting land grants as an established custom, even if contrary to the Laws of the Indies, the magistrate legalized them and dedicated Articles 63 through 82 of his Ordinances to their regulation.

Until November 23, 1729, on which date they were suspended by royal decree—that is, for nearly two centuries—the Cuban councils made use of that exceptional authority to distribute realenga lands among the inhabitants. In this way, numerous great cattle latifundia were created, covering most of the island. This initial development of the latifundium was not and could not be harmful for several reasons. First, since realenga land was abundant and the population scanty, there was land for everyone. Second, the grants were to be used for cattle raising, and the landholders agreed to supply any quantity of beef cattle at prices fixed by the Cabildo. Finally, owing to the foresight of Cáceres, who had been careful to give preference to the concession of lands for agriculture, Articles 70 and 71 provided that to ensure "ample provision grounds" it would be possible to grant land for small farms—known as *estancias*—in any region, even within a holding that had already been assigned to a *hato,* or cattle ranch. The latifundium, therefore, could not obstruct the development of the small-scale proprietor, halt population increase, prevent the extension of agriculture, or hinder the formation of a class of modest independent farmers. Let us make clear, in homage to the memory of that distinguished magistrate, that the safeguard adopted by Cáceres was neither an improvisation nor a happy inspiration. He was already acquainted with the dangers of the sugar latifundium from personal observation; in his excellent *Memoria* addressed to the King in 1570 he had blamed the latifundium for the lack of land devoted to subsistence agriculture in Santo Domingo, stating that land seizure resulted in scarcity and poverty for the majority of the people, who were exploited by a small, wealthy oligarchy.

The process of the allotment and division of Cuban land during the sixteenth, seventeenth, and eighteenth centuries led to the creation of a class of large-scale and small-scale proprietors who were descended from the first settlers and who were deeply attached to their native soil. Mainly a poor, rough people who lived in isolation from the outside world because of the strict laws forbidding any trade or commerce with foreigners, they raised livestock, cultivated small subsistence plots, and occasionally traded hides, salted or cured meat, and other agricultural products with the ships that called at Havana once or twice a year on their way to New Spain or Seville, or with the smugglers of France, Portugal, Holland, and, after the middle of the seventeenth century, Great Britain.

Meanwhile, the rest of the Caribbean, after a brief period during which their white populations developed rapidly, were falling into hopeless decay as the sugar latifundia gradually took over the land and substituted slaves for the small-scale independent farmers. In the British Antilles there were created plantation colonies, no more than factories serving a distant and powerful community; but in Cuba the foundations were laid for a new and original nationhood, the fruit of three centuries of settlement. The different systems of allotment and utilization of the land determined the different destinies of the British and the Spanish Antilles: for the one, decline; for the other, progress, slow but constant.[1]

1. For a detailed study of the origin of landownership and the collective properties or *haciendas comuneras* in Cuba, see R. Guerra, *Historia de Cuba,* vol. 2, pp. 182 ff.

5 Toward the Formation of a Landowning Class in Cuba

> It was not difficult to divide a large property among several sons, nor was it ever difficult to turn cattle ranches into farmland. As the population has increased, these ranches have been divided up and it may be stated that they are now dependent on agriculture.—*Francisco de Arango y Parreño, speech in 1792: "Agriculture in Havana and Ways to Promote It."*

During the second half of the sixteenth, the entire seventeenth, and part of the eighteenth centuries, almost all Cuban territory was covered by cattle ranches, each one extending over thousands of caballerías. Far from

bringing about the destruction of small properties,
which then hardly existed in Cuba, this situation was
the first step toward the process of division and allotment of Cuban land. These latifundia, granted to long-
time inhabitants of the island, encouraged the settlement of vast, unpopulated regions. Since their authorization did not affect the *ejidos* (municipal commons)
of the towns, and since lands could be ceded within
the hatos for estancias and provision grounds, they were
at that time no obstacle at all to an increase in the number of rural properties. They did not signify the seizure
of land by capitalist enterprise, but rather the division
of land among those who occupied it. Such persons
could consider themselves lawful owners and, without
infringing on anyone else's rights, devote themselves
to making the land produce most effectively.

The cattle latifundia were originally individual
grants, but they were almost immediately transformed
into collective properties, the so-called haciendas comuneras. The transformation of the individual latifundium
into a hacienda comunera, held by several people, was
easily accomplished in one of two ways: either by means
of partial property transfers from the first beneficiary
or sole owner, or through its being broken up by inheritance. Very few estates in Cuba were subject to
primogeniture or entailments, owing to the humble
status of the settlers. Sometimes the sole owner of a
cattle latifundium, lacking capital to carry on efficient
production or incentive to continue production in view
of Cuba's commercial isolation, sold a part of his enormous holding or, on his death, left his estate to be
divided among several heirs. In some cases, when a
plantation had not been surveyed because of its im-

mense size, or when it had only one entrance or one source of water for livestock, it was difficult—on occasion, practically impossible—to divide it into two or more equal or proportional parts without engaging in long and costly studies to determine its boundaries, its exact area, its value, and its internal structure. There were few if any surveyors, and the property was seldom of sufficient value to justify the considerable expense involved in the legal formalities of subdividing it.

Given this situation, those who had come to share in the legal possession of a single holding arrived at an agreement—and this practice became the law governing land tenure—for joint benefit from the hato or ranch, and they continued to graze their livestock freely over the entire range. Each *comunero* (proprietor of a joint hacienda) branded or earmarked his livestock, and the wild cattle that could be rounded up, or their hides, were shared proportionally. As the number of comuneros who were legally entitled to participate in each holding gradually increased through successive property transfers and inheritance, the division of the holding into proportional lots became increasingly difficult.

At this point, a much simpler and more efficient procedure was introduced: to appraise the plantation and, instead of a piece of land, to give each of the interested parties a share in the amount at which it had been valued. If the plantation was appraised at four thousand pesos and there were two comuneros with equal rights, each had a share worth two thousand pesos. These shares began to be called *pesos de posesión*. As this practice became general, a given amount of pesos de posesión could be sold, inherited, or transferred in any way.

The transformation of the individual livestock ranch into the hacienda comunera indicates that the social and historical process of subdivision and allotment of land continued without interruption in Cuba. Although the latifundium might remain a large agricultural unit for as much as a century, it was always actually and legally divided into smaller holdings. The immensity of the hatos and ranches, where relatively little livestock grazed, and the limited number of ranchers meant that there was ample space for the comuneros. Because of this, together with the difficulties of legal subdivision, collective ownership lasted a long time.

On the other hand, when it was a question of dissolving the collectivity, there were usually conflicting interests: the comunero with a large amount of pesos de posesión might want to see it ended, whereas the comunero with a minor share might prefer that it continue indefinitely. Nevertheless, perhaps before the close of the sixteenth century, some large holdings were split up for one reason or another, and this was the beginning of the small-scale individual ownership of property.

The sugar industry, which began in Cuba between 1590 and 1600,[1] fifty years before that of Barbados, helped for more than a century and a half to accelerate the division of the cattle ranches and to increase the number of Cuban rural proprietors. In the first place, the sugar industry was not promoted from abroad by merchants, as had happened in Barbados; there the Dutch offered sugar mill equipment and African slaves in exchange for sugar and developed a doubly profitable trade. In Cuba the industry was developed from

1. See *Historia de Cuba,* vol. 2, pp. 248 ff.

within by the country's inhabitants, who lived in great poverty and searched eagerly for new sources of livelihood. However, the first initiative did come from abroad—from Mexico—in the form of a Crown loan which was granted to the farmers by Philip II at the request of the Havana Cabildo and supported by the governor of the island. From the beginning, the sugar mills were extended protection against foreclosure for debt, an extremely important privilege that was considered an indispensable aid to this new industry. For the planting of cane, the Havana Cabildo itself ceded lands, within a radius of eight leagues, that had been reserved for growing food crops. Thus, the first sugar mills were set up very close to the municipal limits and were owned by the wealthiest and most influential colonists.

The new industry, despite the Crown loan and the great privileges it enjoyed, grew very slowly because of insurmountable obstacles: the lack of markets and the difficulties of importing equipment and slaves. The Laws of the Indies cut Cuba off completely from foreign trade and limited its traffic with Spain to the single port of Seville, to which the Spanish colonies of the New World were linked by only one expedition a year; this fleet touched at Havana with scanty cargo space available, and that went at a very high fee. Spain, a nation which had been in pronounced decline since the beginning of the seventeenth century, offered little market for the sugar of the Indies because its consumption was meager and because cane had been planted and sugar manufactured in some parts of Granada since the time of Arab domination. Copper vessels to boil the cane juice, or *guarapo,* in the sugar mills and clay pots in which to cure the sugar could not be imported directly from Portugal or the other countries where they were manufactured, but had to make a long and costly detour through Seville, by which time they had passed through so many hands that they became very expensive. Add to this the fact that the importation of slaves into the Indies was always a monopoly, licensed to private companies by the Spanish kings and subject to numerous restrictions and heavy duties, and it is understandable that an industry producing sugar at high cost and with a limited market could not prosper.

The industry grew so slowly that during the four-year period ending in 1763, when it had been operating for one hundred and fifty years, annual sugar exports were less than 21,000 *arrobas* (the *arroba* is 25.35 pounds or 11.5 kilograms), according to the estimates of Don Francisco de Arango y Parreño.

Writers have long pointed out that Cuba was deliberately excluded from commerce by the Laws of the Indies in order to satisfy the interests of the Spanish treasury and Seville merchants. However, by preventing a sudden expansion of the sugar industry for two centuries, these same circumstances hampered the development of slavery and the sugar latifundium, and guaranteed that Cuban society would have a gradual internal growth based on a white population that owned and tilled its native soil.

With the seventeenth century a new commercial crop, tobacco, was introduced into Cuba. After this product had come into use all over Europe, it was discovered that Cuba was exceptionally well suited to the cultivation of high-grade tobacco. The relatively light labor involved in growing and handling it and the small amount of capital required helped tobacco farms to flourish and spread in spite of restrictions and monopolies. Tobacco farming developed within and at the expense of the hacienda comunera and was one more factor contributing to the break-up of the cattle latifundium. By the middle of the eighteenth century there were many farms devoted to tobacco, which, with cattle and sugar, became one of the mainstays of the Cuban economy.

But this slow and obscure growth of a Cuba isolated and nearly forgotten by the world was to come to an end. The two great upheavals of the eighteenth century —the English industrial revolution of 1750–60 and the French Revolution of 1789—accelerated the tempo of life everywhere; even in Cuba, far removed from the scene of these events, they created new living and working conditions that would soon complete the formation of our national identity.

6   The Development of an
Agrarian Society in Cuba

> It would perhaps be difficult to find another
> country of America that can compare with
> Cuba in the number of landowners instructed
> in the theory and art of agriculture, and as
> aware of the changes that should be intro-
> duced to ensure their country's steady prog-
> ress toward higher production and prosper-
> ity.—*Report of the Cuban Commissioners to
> the Information Board, 1866.*

The capture of Havana and its occupation for a number of months by the English in 1762, just as steam-
driven machinery was about to usher in the industrial
revolution; the easing of the Spanish trade restrictions

on Cuba during the reign of Charles III and the increased communication between the two countries with more frequent shipping service; the creation of a great free market near Cuba, with the establishment of the United States in 1776; and the destruction of Haiti's sugar and coffee wealth in the decade following 1790, which was one of the consequences of the French Revolution in the Antilles—all these events conspired to draw Cuba out of the isolation into which it had been forced by the Laws of the Indies and to thrust it into the turmoil of the outside world. Cuba's slow growth over the years, based almost exclusively upon the natural increase of its original white settlers, gave way to a rapid development of all its sources of wealth and to an influx of thousands of African slaves. To open the doors to progress was, by one of those strange contradictions of history, to put Cuba on the road toward becoming just one more plantation colony. However, powerful forces were to spare Cuba that misfortune for more than a century and to grant it the opportunity to become a free and civilized country in the Caribbean—proving that the wretched fate of the other islands was the result of human greed, and not of some inescapable geographical determinism.

The English, during the months they occupied Havana and for most of their jurisdiction, opened the port to trade with England and its colonies and flooded Cuba with African slaves. Buyers for Cuban sugar and the influx of low-priced slaves—it is believed that approximately 10,000 slaves were brought into Cuba at that time—were incentives to expansion of the industry. When the island was returned to Spain this movement continued, but at a slower pace, owing to the restriction of its market to Spain once again, the lack of capital, the higher price of slaves, and various other reasons discussed by Don Francisco Arango y Parreño in his admirable *Discurso Sobre la Agricultura de la Habana y Medios de Fomentarla* in 1792.

In the last quarter of the eighteenth century Cuba had a population of 96,440 whites, 31,847 free colored, and 44,333 slaves in its 44,000 square miles of territory. Barbados, with only 166 square miles, had 62,115 slaves; Haiti, the wealthy French colony, with an area of 11,000 square miles, had 38,000 white inhabitants and 452,000 slaves. In the Western Atlantic, Barbados and Haiti had become slave depots, but Cuba was the nucleus of a kind of society for which a better fate seemed reserved. Rural properties continued to multiply, and the census showed 339 large cattle ranches; 7,814 small properties including pastures, farmlands, tobacco fields, and estancias; and 478 sugar mills, more than twice as many as existed a few years before the capture of Havana by the English.

But Cuban agriculture was given its decisive impetus by the destruction of Haiti's riches in the slave uprisings of 1789. The sugar latifundium created so precarious a social structure in Haiti and inflicted such grievous suffering upon the slave population that as soon as the mother country, convulsed with internal revolutionary struggles, momentarily relaxed its coercive grip, the slaves rose in revolt. A catastrophe ensued which in a few months ruined the economy of this wealthy colony, principal supplier of Europe's sugar and coffee. The prices of both articles shot up, initiating in 1790 a period of prosperity, perhaps the most famous in Cuban history, which lasted almost a decade.

Arango y Parreño, who heard the news of the Haitian uprising in Madrid, realized that Cuba could profit enormously from this situation. Acting as representative of the Havana *Ayuntamiento* (municipal government), he secured the free importation of slaves, several important benefits for the farmers, and the elimination of many trade barriers. He thus cleared the way for production to surge ahead, thanks to the market created by the newly independent United States that absorbed most of our goods and the naval wars of the French Revolution that kept Spain so isolated that, very unwillingly, it was compelled to permit Cuban trade with neutral countries. Cuba grasped the scepter that Haiti had let fall; and a broad expanse of forests was rapidly leveled by fire and axe to make room for fields of sugar cane, coffee, and tobacco. Meanwhile, over a period of thirty years, frequent expeditions from Havana to the Guinea coasts had multiplied the number of slaves sixfold and reduced the white population to a minority of 40 per cent.

The sudden increase in Cuban wealth, however, did not encourage the development of the latifundium. On the contrary, it hastened the dissolution of the cattle latifundia and increased the number of small and medium-sized rural properties. In the first place, many farmers were drawn away from sugar cane agriculture by the high prices of coffee and tobacco, products whose marketability benefited greatly from the abolition of state monopoly. And since the sugar mills at that time had to maintain large numbers of oxen and subsistence lands to feed their field hands, the production of livestock and food crops could never be neglected. The demand for land, as much for agriculture as for the settlement of new towns, was enormous, and it became essential to dissolve the haciendas comuneras and to subdivide individually owned cattle latifundia. A large sugar mill required, at the most, forty caballerías of land; a coffee hacienda, much less; and the tobacco fields and estancias, still less; so it was inevitable that cattle latifundia would have to be subdivided. The ranch owners, under some pressure, did not resist because, as Arango y Parreño wrote,

> It is a happy day for the owner of the cattle ranch when he can sell his land to be used for agriculture. From this grazing land which was worth 16,000 to 20,000 pesos, he is going to earn 300,000 to 400,000 pesos by selling it in caballerías for sugar mills, cassava fields, or pastures.

While individual interest welcomed the termination of the hacienda comunera and the division of the great rural landed estates, the Spanish government, far from keeping itself aloof, wholeheartedly encouraged and aided this vital movement in several ways. First, the general and extraordinary parliamentary sessions of 1813, in a January 4 decree, ordered that all idle and realenga lands be converted into private property. One portion was to be distributed in the form of rewards to those who had served their country; another was to be distributed among those inhabitants who had no land and wanted some; and the rest was to be sold on easy terms, the returns to be used for payment of the national debt. Second, provisions were made to guarantee to the proprietor free and perpetual possession of his land and, if he acted in good faith, all questions concerning title were to be settled in his favor. Finally, on April 1,

1819, the decision of the Audiencia of Puerto Príncipe [Cuba] was approved, establishing an easy, rapid, and economical procedure for the division of the hacienda comunera, subject to prior claims of community ownership. Therefore, during the first two decades of the nineteenth century numerous haciendas comuneras were dissolved and many latifundia were partitioned, thanks to promotion by private interests and energetic assistance from the colonial government.

At the very time when the whole continent was rising up against Spain, there was originating in Cuba the largest, hardiest, most prosperous, and most enterprising class of rural proprietors in its history. The 1827 census, taken under Vives, recorded for the island 1,000 sugar mills, 2,067 coffee haciendas, 76 cotton farms, 66 cocoa plantations, 3,090 ranches, 5,534 tobacco farms, and 13,947 subsistence farms and estancias. Less favorable were the data on population—a total of 704,487 inhabitants, of whom 311,051 were free white, 286,942 slaves, and the rest free colored. But, as has been seen, even though economic development had led to an increase in the colored population (mainly slaves), it had not brought about a concentration of property but had instead encouraged its division and increased the number of proprietors. Cuban agrarian society was firmly established, and Cuba could count on thousands of solidly united families, attached to their own soil and personally directing its cultivation —a generally prosperous people, anxious for progress, for political autonomy, and for the opportunity to serve their country.

From the class of rural landowners came the Aguilera, Céspedes, Maceo Osorio, Figueredo, Cisneros

Betancourt, Aldama, Morales Lemus, Frías, Mazorra, Alfonso, Agramonte, Echeverría, Iznaga, and other families in that long series of distinguished citizens who have shaped Cuba economically, socially, and politically. They were a hard-working, enterprising people who were widely traveled and who sent their children to school in France and England. In the Economic Society, the Agricultural, Industrial, and Commercial Consulates, the Development Board, the Information Board, during the Yara Revolution, and in the Autonomist Party, they made memorable efforts to guarantee that Cuba should have the social and governmental institutions and the public liberties that are the crowning achievement of any group effort toward progress and civilization.

7 Cuban Sugar Mills
Without Latifundia

Although, thanks to conditions that are now
changing, the island has managed to maintain
a certain equilibrium between agricultural
expenditures and yields, it has also been able
to increase production by hard work and by
using the latest methods of sugar cane cultivation and sugar manufacture.—*Report of
the Cuban Commissioners to the Information
Board, 1866: Proposal on the Economic
Problem.*

The sugar industry, tremendously stimulated by the
sudden rise in prices that followed the destruction of

Haiti's wealth between 1790 and 1800, was assisted by the opportune intervention of Arango y Parreño, who obtained for Cuba the free importation of slaves, the liberalizing of trade, and other important benefits. Nonetheless, the expansion of the industry was never conducive to the development of the latifundium for reasons that permit an interesting and suggestive contrast with the present situation.

In the first place, high prices thrust not only Cuba but the British West Indies and other regions into sugar cultivation, and by 1800 overproduction had depressed and demoralized the market. The sugar boom, as it would be known today, ended; and since the price of coffee, a product which cannot be produced in a short time, remained high, much agricultural effort was reoriented to its planting. The abrupt fall in the price of sugar at the beginning of the century ruined more than thirty Cuban sugar mills, and the sugar industry began to experience what the English called the "lottery of the West Indies." Mill owners had just begun to recover from this first disaster when the United States, during the French and English wars, declared an embargo (1807). With North American ports closed to foreign trade and North American ships (the principal carriers of Cuban sugar) prevented from sailing, production suffered another blow.

But the second decade of the nineteenth century had not ended before the mill owners saw the industry threatened by two new clouds on the horizon. The first was the appearance of a fearful competitor, beet sugar, the perfection of which Napoleon had energetically promoted during the blockade of the continent. Although the new industry owed its origin to pressures resulting from the necessities of war, it created powerful interests that engaged in an all-out battle against sugar cane during the rest of the century. The second threat was the legal suppression of slave traffic in a treaty imposed by England upon Spain in 1817. It was to become effective in 1821 and signified an attempt by England to destroy Cuba's ruinous competition with the British West Indies.

Its growth already checked by these factors, the industry's expansion continued to be blocked by great difficulties of a more or less permanent nature. In 1818 Cuba was granted permission to trade with all foreign countries. But the discriminatory three-column tariff imposed by Spanish mercantile interests to protect the mother country's production and navy; the exceedingly high rate of interest on loans, originating in the lack of banks; and the prohibitive cost of insurance at a time when Spain, almost without a navy, was fighting its rebellious colonies burdened the sugar planters so heavily that the cultivation of sugar cane could never threaten to absorb all of the productive energy of the country.

By 1820 mill owners were faced with the serious problem of substituting steam-driven machinery for their traditional milling methods. Such machinery had first appeared in the English textile industry in the middle of the eighteenth century and had spread to other activities, including sugar manufacture. From the beginning of the century attempts were made to introduce it into Cuba, and before the end of the second decade of the nineteenth century there were already steam-driven mills in many parts of the island. After 1820 the competition of the sugar beet forced the industry to run its rollers by steam and to use improved equipment for clarifying juice.

With the introduction of steam-driven machinery, sugar mills began to grow in size, and within a century they had changed from modest sugar works into the gigantic million-bag central factories of today. However, for the first seventy years of the century sugar mills grew slowly, not only because of the unfavorable conditions already mentioned, but because of other material obstacles to the development of large factories, such as lack of internal transportation, the problem of providing fuel, and the need for huge teams of oxen to cart the cane and sugar.

Cane and, to a lesser extent, sugar are heavy and bulky. In a country without highways or good roads, and before the invention of the railroad, it was very costly to transport cane and sugar long distances in primitive carts. For this reason the sugar mill could not be built at too great a remove from the fields which supplied it, and the sugar latifundium in the modern sense remained a physical impossibility. The railway, which first appeared in England in 1826, was introduced into Cuba ten years later by companies organized or backed by mill owners, but only for the transportation of sugar to coastal ports. It was still not profitable to transport cane by railroad.

Another factor preventing a great expansion of the sugar mill was its enormous consumption of fuel. For each *zafra*—cane harvesting and grinding period—entire forests were laid waste, and the supply of firewood, because of transportation difficulties, could not be located very far from the sugar mill. Many yokes of oxen were required for hauling cane, firewood, and sugar, as well as for tilling and planting the fields. The larger its capacity, the more pasture land the mill was obliged to maintain for livestock that remained largely idle in the "dead season." And since slave labor was used, hundreds of workers had to be lodged, clothed, fed, and given medical attention all year round. This meant that a vast amount of essential invested capital was unproductive for periods of several months. All these conditions explain why the Cuban sugar plant was limited in size until the middle of the century.

For half a century rural property continued to develop, and the sugar industry was extended principally by an increase in the number of sugar mills. In 1827 there were 1,000 mills; in 1846, according to reliable data, there were 1,442; and in 1860 Pezuela estimated that large and small mills totaled 2,000, perhaps the greatest number in Cuba's history. By this last date, some sugar mills had become very large in spite of the problems of expansion. In a list of twenty-two important mills which appears in Pezuela's *Diccionario Geográfico, Estadístico e Histórico de la Isla de Cuba* only one sugar refinery, the Santa Susana in Cienfuegos, had an area of as much as 340 caballerías. It was followed in size by the San Martín (222 caballerías) owned by Don Francisco Pedroso y Herrera; most of the others were in the neighborhood of 45, 56, or 58 caballerías in size.

It is not strange that production, still exclusively based on Cuban capital, should rise rather slowly and should follow *pari passu* the general development of the country in population, wealth, communications, and real income. In the first five years of the century annual sugar exports averaged, according to Pezuela,

2,964,064 arrobas and in the five-year period ending in 1840 they averaged 10,148,555. If it is borne in mind that Cuba's population had increased considerably, that free trade had existed since 1818, and that railroad and steamship transportation offered facilities unknown twenty years earlier, it may be concluded that the industry's growth was moderate, in proportion to other aspects of national production, and contributing to the country's wealth by increasing the number of properties as well as the number of prosperous rural landowners. It is a fact that in the first half of the century the Cuban planter was very active not only in increasing his personal wealth but also in promoting his country's general welfare.

Mill owners were hard-working members of the Economic Society and the Development Board; mill owners persuaded Father Varela y Saco to initiate the teaching of physics and chemistry in Cuba, in order to meet the needs of the sugar industry; mill owners brought over the chemist, Casaseca, and founded our first botanical garden; mill owners imported steam-driven machinery to run sugar mill rollers and, as we have said, also organized our first public service railway companies; and finally, mill owners, in addition to drafting and sponsoring all the economic, social, and political reforms instituted in Cuba during the first two decades of the century, vigorously advocated the immigration of white settlers, and the most determined and honorable among them persisted in their efforts despite the threats and slanders of the slave traders—contrabandists who maintained profitable and usually clandestine relations with high colonial authorities.

This attitude and line of conduct were maintained

by influential Cubans of that period because they were acquainted with the history of the British West Indies, and they energetically rejected such a future for their homeland.

> We do not know [said the Cuban Commissioners to the Information Board of 1866, in reply to one of the questionnaires submitted to them by the Spanish government] if the foreign Antilles, where other population principles have prevailed and continue to do so, are destined to any future other than that of great factories where tropical crops are raised and processed by the labor of non-white races, or that of simple trading stations for the mother country's shipping; but no one who understands the political, economic, and social importance of the islands that Spain still owns in these waters, could wish for them so secondary a future, so subordinate a role in the charter of modern civilization. Cuba, at least, which is much larger than the other islands, and which has the ingredients needed to raise it to a higher destiny, should at no time sacrifice those ingredients to the fictitious or transitory conveniences of a commercialism without foresight or dignity.

As those men thought and felt, so should we think about the commercialism "without foresight or dignity" of today's latifundium.

Part Three

The Development of the
Sugar Latifundium in Cuba

8 Background of the Latifundium Period

Agriculture may be separated from milling in two ways: the cane fields and the refinery and other equipment used in sugar processing may belong to the same or to different persons. If to the same person, the owner may divide his lands among colonos and either pay them a salary for their labor or give them a share of the crop. This method has many advantages because small lots of land will be better farmed; if the year is bad, the plantation owner will save the wages he would otherwise have to pay; and since the colono is not limited to a fixed salary, he will be eager to farm better so that the cane will

yield more, because his earnings will be proportionate to the size of his crop.—*Report
of the mill owner Don Domingo Aldama to
General Serrano, in opposition to an African
colonization plan in 1862.*

From 1840 to 1860 sugar production increased rapidly
in Cuba, and sugar exports rose from 12,867,698 arrobas for the five years from 1841 through 1845 to
23,139,245 arrobas for the period 1856 through 1859,
according to Pezuela. This rapid development was assisted by a fall in the price of coffee which almost completely ruined the coffee plantations. Consequently,
almost all of the farms, capital, and labor that had been
engaged in coffee cultivation were turned to the production of sugar. In other words, the sugar industry
was strengthened by the destruction of one of the
economy's four pillars—livestock, sugar cane, tobacco,
and coffee. Coffee, although the last to appear, had
come to be one of the strongest and most prosperous.

Meanwhile, advances in processing methods and
mechanical improvements forced constant renewal of
machinery and other factory installations in the sugar
mills. They expanded continually and were already
enterprises requiring large amounts of capital. It became necessary to abandon the old practice whereby
each farmer, no matter how few caballerías he had
planted, would set up his own grinding mill for his
cane; by 1850 or 1860 the number of mills had leveled
off. Future development would occur no longer through
an increase in the number of mills but through an increase in the capacity of each. It was no longer possible
to be a sugar planter without being a large landowner

or capitalist. Small sugar mills, less effective in cane juice extraction and often producing sugar of lower quality, could not meet the competition and, at first barely surviving, began to fail and disappear. Many were destroyed during the Ten Years' War. For example, in 1862 in the Bayamo area there were twenty-four sugar mills, including one steam-driven; in the Manzanillo area there were six steam-driven mills out of a total of eighteen. In 1877 not a single mill was recorded for these areas, and around Holguín they had been reduced from sixteen to only four. The number of sugar mills fell from 2,000 in 1860 to 1,190 in 1877.

One of the first effects of this twofold process—reduction in the number of sugar mills and increase in the manufacturing capacity of those that continued to operate—was the appearance of a new type of producer, the colono,[1] who planted cane but did not own a mill to grind and convert it into sugar. Instead, he had his cane ground at the nearest sugar mill and, paying the owner with part of his product, disposed of the rest as he wished.[2] The colono symbolized the division of the production of sugar into separate growing and processing phases and the decline of the traditional planter who also processed and sold his sugar. Nevertheless, farmers continued to be independent producers. They had their cane ground at the mills under specified

1. For the variations in meaning of this term, see the Glossary.

2. "The custom traditionally followed was always that of assigning to the sugar-cane producer the right to receive a certain number of arrobas of sugar—more or less, according to the situation, or the actual value thereof, in line with the market price, for each hundred arrobas of cane delivered to the mill"—Ramiro Guerra y Sánchez, *La Industria Azucarera de Cuba* (Imprenta Cultural, Havana, 1940), p. 37.

conditions and received a share of the sugar to dispose of on whatever terms they could get. Mills that received cane from independent farmers in these circumstances came to be called *centrales* at the end of the Ten Years' War. The existence of the central and the system of colonos date approximately from that time.

This new arrangement came about spontaneously to meet the needs of both the mill owners and the farmer turned colono. In the 1850s and 1860s mill owners were hampered by the lack of the capital they required to modernize and expand their factory machinery and by the size of their mills, which presented enormous problems of organization and administration. The Count of Pozos Dulces and other economists of that period advanced the principle of division of labor as a means for solving the industry's problems: sugar manufacture and agriculture should be kept distinct and separate. By devoting himself exclusively to processing, the manufacturer would reduce the extent of his enterprise and could employ all his capital in improving, enlarging, and operating the mill. He would free himself from the immense expense and burden of seeing to the purchase of lands and the cultivation of cane and its transportation to the factory. The mill owner never completely gave up growing sugar cane but, adapting his financial and administrative problems to the problems of the farmer who could not afford to maintain a mill, he began to grind his neighbors' cane and charge for this service in sugar. This opened a new era in the history of the sugar industry by creating and extending a new social class, the colono, which has slowly but surely become economically dependent on the central.

The establishment of the central and colono system at first did not lead to the appearance of the latifundium, but delayed it instead. If the expanding central had not been supplied by the colono, its stock of cane would have had to be ensured by land purchases and farm administration, in spite of capital shortages and the scarcity of labor after the abolition of slavery. Mills could be and were enlarged, therefore, without additional farm land. Although mills were becoming huge, there was no over-all movement in the direction of the latifundium. Subdivision of properties continued at a slower rate, creating "cane colonies," and at the end of the century there was a total of 60,711 farms in cane, representing 30 per cent of Cuba's total area. The general obstacles to rapid development have been enumerated and, still existing, they stood in the way of the latifundium.

After 1868 another powerful obstacle was added: the insecure conditions for capital and business, especially outside the cities, during the long and bloody wars of independence. Production developed very slowly and even suffered serious setbacks, for example in the years 1885–90, when it was much lower than in 1870–75.

But before the close of the nineteenth century and the end of Spanish rule in Cuba, a new factor came into play that is mainly responsible for the latifundium: the competition among the mills for their raw material, sugar cane.

Mills had not competed with each other formerly because each was limited to a circumscribed area by the lack of adequate and economical transportation. No mill invaded the lands of its neighbor mill, and more than a hundred small mills might be contained in one municipal district.

As mills grew into centrales they required a much greater supply of cane. Although the supply area was constantly being expanded, its boundaries were set by the high cost of carting; but in 1836 the introduction of the railroad finally resulted in bitter competition among the centrales and eventually brought about the latifundium. Until 1878 the railroads developed slowly all over the world because, in spite of their enormous advantages, they were an expensive and still imperfect means of transportation. But after 1870, when iron rails began to be replaced by steel and the price of steel rails in the United States decreased from $106 per ton in 1870 to $44 in 1878, railroads developed amazingly and came into wide use.

The centrales of Cuba, consuming more and more cane as they grew in size, began to lay down their own narrow gauge tracks, which enabled them to bring cane to the mill at moderate cost from regions previously outside the central area. At the same time, the network of public railways made it feasible to move cane over long distances. In theory, the central could now expand endlessly but, in practice, for long hauls the zone of each factory was circumscribed by the expense of laying lines or by freight charges.

From the moment a central was able to invade another's traditional supply area, rivalry between the two was inevitable. At first there an increase in the amount of sugar offered the colono in exchange for grinding his cane and, until a few years ago, it was still possible to identify these competing zones by the higher number of arrobas of sugar that the farmer received from the central for his cane. In Havana, Matanzas, and Santa Clara, where there were many centrales and a public railroad promoting their rivalry, the colono was free to sell his cane to the highest bidder and was given more than seven arrobas of sugar for every hundred of cane. In Camagüey, Oriente, and parts of Pinar del Río, where there were no railroads, only four—or at the most, five and a half—were offered.

Competition created a new problem for the centrales: how to guarantee that each would have enough cane for each zafra at the lowest possible cost. This could be accomplished through one of two means: by economic domination of the colono—reducing his independence and making him a vassal of the mill, bound by contract and prevented from freely selling his product—or by purchasing lands and administering them as cane farms or having them sharecropped or rented by colonos dependent on the mill.

The first means twisted the original colono system by changing a class of free farmers into feudal vassals of the central; the second led directly to the latifundium by destroying small and medium-sized rural properties and replacing the old-style colono with either a kind of unpaid employee whose earnings would derive from his farming of lands owned and financed by the mill and under its strict supervision and accounting or, in the case of "administration" farming, with a day laborer.

This marked the beginning of the contest between colono and central. The last decades of the century passed without any appreciable change in the situation because the capital resources of each continued to be fairly evenly matched. But independence created new conditions for industry and, through the Cuban government's lack of foresight, permitted foreign capital to weigh overwhelmingly on the side of the factory.

9 Preparing the Ground for the Latifundium

Article 1. From this date it is strictly forbidden to make any contract or agreement by which property is transferred to foreigners. . . .

Article 6. No foreigner or foreign organization, of any type or category, may establish settlements, villages and towns without first having obtained the authorization of the Congress of the Republic by demonstrating the necessity or desirability of such establishments.

Article 7. The settlements, villages and towns established with the authorization referred to in the foregoing Article shall be governed by the laws of the Republic.

Article 8. Any settlement of more than 250 persons attached to a sugar mill, sugar factory or any other rural farm shall be incorporated into the nearest municipality, to be considered within its jurisdiction and governed by the Ordinances and provisions that it may issue or that may be in force.— *Draft law presented by Senator Manuel Sanguily, dated March 3, 1903,* Congressional Journal, *Vol. 2, No. 40, Havana, November 1908. It never reached debate.*

With the end of Spanish rule in Cuba, very favorable conditions were created for the development of the sugar industry. Some were general and affected business as a whole, others were related only to the sugar sector; but all in one way or another contributed to the transformation of the central into the immense modern latifundium.

Once the country was at peace, it became safe for business. Absolute guarantees were offered capital investment not only by the Cuban government but also by the formidable strength of the United States. The terms of the Treaty of Paris, which in 1898 ended the Spanish-American War, and the Permanent Treaty between Cuba and the United States, drawn up in accordance with the Platt Amendment, ended the fear of revolutionary damage and eliminated one of the obstacles that had inhibited foreign investment in Cuba since the middle of the nineteenth century.

Another very important consideration was the conquest of yellow fever and the extraordinary improvement in sanitary conditions. From a disease-ridden island which took a high toll in foreign lives, Cuba was transformed into a healthy country with a low mortality rate. Precautions against epidemics were strictly enforced, and measures were taken to combat them at the first outbreak.

Also, because of its interest in railway development, the government gave generous subsidies to the railroad companies, as well as to other public utilities enterprises, thus helping to open up new and extensive regions to development through the initiative of organizers and entrepreneurs. At the same time, the lowering of most of the customs barriers, formerly designed to protect the interests of Spain against the trade of the rest of the world, offered opportunities hitherto unknown to foreign commerce.

Finally, investment of foreign capital was welcomed as a demonstration of faith in the Republic and special laws were enacted for banks and their branches, which were subject to minimal state control and paid insignificant taxes. These were but the most salient factors that contributed effectively to opening Cuba to the unhindered activity of capitalist enterprise. In Cuba such enterprise was free from any of the restrictions placed on it in the United States itself, the land of big business, by the Sherman antitrust laws and all the other regulations for maintaining a sound balance among the various forces behind industrial, financial, and commercial development.

Aside from the influence of these general causes, the sugar industry received a powerful stimulus from the Reciprocal Treaty clause which reduced by 20 per cent the United States tariff on Cuban sugar. Cuba is better located than any other sugar-producing country to sell its commodity to the United States. During the colonial period, customs barriers separated Cuba from its neighbor. But when that wall was not only demolished but replaced by a treaty that gave Cuba special privileges in the United States tariff system, foreign capital interested in the sugar industry decided that Cuba was an ideal country for investment.

Also of special and direct interest to the mills was the railroad legislation enacted by the military government of General Wood, which has provided and still provides exceptional facilities for the construction of private railways. When a private railway dominates a region, it inevitably outstrips the public railroad by depriving it of its most important freight and therefore eliminates competition. It also aids the mills in the endless expansion by which they become absolute masters of the landowner or farmer, who lacks economical transportation for his products The government's concession of the so-called *subpuertos* (private coastal piers) was to give the private railway a final advantage. By guaranteeing to each central exclusive transportation for domestic and foreign trade, the subpuertos not only permitted great economies but protected the central against all competition in its particular zone.

Opposing these very favorable conditions for the development of a powerful sugar industry was only one measure that, by relating its growth to the country's increase in population, could restrict its drive or contain its force. This was the wise and provident legislation, enacted under General Wood, which limited so-called undesirable immigration. Promoted energetically and with patriotic zeal by the Cuban public from the time of Saco and Pozos Dulces, its inclusion in the Reciprocal Treaty of 1902 was insisted upon by North American beet sugar interests. But this obstacle was easily overcome by the most powerful companies, when it was a question of their making more money at the expense of the Cuban worker and of national welfare.[1] Who would have imagined that Cuba's presidents and ministers of state, almost all of them men of the revolution, with their special permits to contract for and import Haitians and Jamaicans, would vindicate the captains-general O'Donnell, Roncali, Cañedo, and Concha, who, little more than fifty years before, had facilitated the traffic of slave dealers on the grounds that the cultivation of cane made the slaves indispensable! The complicity of these governors, said to be purchased at the rate of an ounce of gold for each slave, was always held up to Spain by Cuban revolutionaries as one of the most shameful aspects of the colonial period and as one of the most heinous crimes committed against Cuba by Spain in its effort to continue dominating our country.

Wood's measure has now been amended by the highest Cuban authorities, who no doubt mistakenly believe that they are serving the best interests of the national economy. But it is sad to reflect that all the past thinking, writing, and efforts of Cuba's most eminent statesmen and patriots have been in vain, and that public

1. North American beet sugar growers foresaw that the treaty would encourage rapid growth of the Cuban sugar industry, in competition with their own. Therefore, as a condition of the treaty's approval by the United States Senate, they demanded that importation of cheap labor into Cuba be limited so that the industry would grow slowly. General Wood, who was in complete charge of the government of Cuba, had the law promulgated as a military order.

and high government circles are so slow to realize certain truths which are basic to the country's security and welfare but are outweighed by powerful material influences when they are placed on the scale of national destinies.[2]

With the country opened up to world progress and swept clean of the last obstructions of the colonial period, with extraordinary incentives and the elimination of the only possible hindrance to its growth, the sugar industry could and did extend itself by using the two invincible courses of action employed in Barbados: very cheap labor and foreign capital in search of profit. It consolidated itself in about 180 sugar mills and more than 170,000 caballerías of property, a fifth of the national territory and perhaps more than half the arable land of Cuba. In addition, it controlled many more caballerías, either by renting them or by isolating them within the mills' zones of influence.

But precisely here lies Cuba's tragedy. For four centuries its people had been settling the country little by little, clearing it and making it a healthy place to live in. They imported its principal commercial crops; they adapted cattle and domestic livestock to its climate; they found suitable locations for towns and cities on its coasts and in its interior; they courageously defended the island against invasion; they allotted and divided its land among farmers; they laid out and built its modern railways as well as its old but useful country roads; they fought for liberty and independence in the hope of establishing a vigorous republic that would be shared by and would serve all; and, thanks to the genius of a

2. Since the first edition of this book, immigration of cheap labor has been restricted by law. [Note to the third edition.]

Cuban—Finlay—not only Cuba but the whole world was freed of one of its worst plagues.

When all this toil of centuries seemed to be almost completed and the fruits could at last be enjoyed by their children, the sugar latifundium, which had ruined the West Indies with its two formidable instruments, foreign capital and imported cheap labor, invaded the island. Its appearance marked the beginning of the wholesale destruction of our small and medium-sized properties and the reduction of our rural landowners and independent farmers, backbone of our nation, to the lowly condition of a proletariat being stifled by that economic asphyxiation which afflicts the country today from one end to the other.

10 The Latifundium in Full Flower

As this authentic economic revolution develops, it will be followed by a social and
political revolution; that is, the transformation of our territorial wealth through changing ownership will result in powerful foreign
influences on our daily life. Our language will
become eroded, discredited and adulterated.
Ultimately, Cuba will be confronted with
frightful legal problems and complications
which it will be useless to lament and which
we shall be powerless to solve, and we shall
suffer the painful loss of our national integrity.—*Manuel Sanguily: Paragraph from
the draft law submitted to the Senate on
March 3, 1903,* Congressional Journal, *Vol.
2, No. 40, Havana, November 1908.*

Already underway in the last years of Spanish domination and encouraged after 1899 by the circumstances described in the preceding chapter, the rapid development of the sugar latifundium in Cuba was brought about, as in Barbados in the middle of the seventeenth century, by the sudden stimulus of a foreign financial power and the importation of low-cost labor; and its purpose was identical. It did not seek to promote the welfare or the material and moral advancement of the people of a cane-growing country, but was entirely dedicated to obtaining a high profit on invested capital. By supplying sugar at a very low price to the consumer, the producer country becomes an economic fief of a distant metropolis, and its working class lives in poverty so that the country that dominates and exploits it can live better and more cheaply.

In Barbados, foreign financial power was represented by Dutch merchants, its imported low-cost labor by African slaves, the exploiter countries by the great commercial firms of London and Holland, and the immediate stimulus to its sugar enterprise by the domestic upheavals in England, which left the seas open for a number of years to the Dutch navy. In Cuba, financial power has come from the United States—mainly banks and refineries—cheap labor has been and continues to be Haitian and Jamaican, the metropolis benefited has been first of all the United States, and the immediate and direct cause of the latifundium's sudden growth was the high price of sugar owing to war in Europe. Cuba alone, with its own capital and labor force, could not have extended the industry to the point where it would have altered Cuban society at large. Nor with moderate prices for sugar would the industry have increased with such excessive speed.

According to the census of 1899, the number of sugar mills in operating condition had been reduced to 207 from 1,190 in 1877, as the result of the ruin of many small mills between 1877 and 1895 and the destruction created by the Wars of Independence. The *Times of Cuba,* June 15, 1927, states that 185 mills ground cane in the last zafra. As may be seen, sugar mills have continued to decrease in number, with twenty-two fewer now than in 1899; it is certain that the sugar industry will continue to concentrate and that several more centrales will disappear. However, the centrales have enormously increased their capacity to the point that one factory can process a million bags of thirteen arrobas' weight in the short period of four or five months.

Cuba has experienced the universal phenomenon of industrial concentration, which makes possible cheap production by reducing overhead expenses and proportionately cutting the cost per unit and which also eliminates competition. This has been accompanied by a rush to acquire the land adjoining the sugar mill in order to have available a cheap supply of raw material. It may be thought that industrial concentration was adopted by the centrales as a natural means of defense against foreign competition. But taking over and administering land for cane cultivation was a direct attack on the Cuban farmer who could still obtain a greater amount of sugar for each hundred arrobas of cane wherever there was a public railroad.

For the people of Cuba, this is the most important feature of the entire economic process under examination. The central monopolized lands for the exclusive purpose of subjugating the farmer, of forcing him into submission; he was told to plant cane exactly as he was instructed or to abandon his farm and go somewhere else. On a map of Cuba showing the percentage of arrobas of sugar given by the mill to the farmer for every hundred arrobas of cane, the highest figures would indicate the zones where sugar mills still competed for cane and the lowest figures would correspond to the zones where all rivalry had disappeared and where the colono received only enough sugar to induce him to continue planting cane for the central, until such time as he might be evicted in favor of a cheaper method of cane farming.

It is said that the latifundium is indispensable to the existence of the sugar industry. This is an error. The latifundium is indispensable to the domination and exploitation of the colono by the central, which can then set its own conditions; that is, it enables forty, or at the most fifty, companies to control hundreds of thousands of farmers; but it is not essential to the planting or processing of cane. There are more just and humane bases upon which to organize sugar production. If there were not, Cuba would have no interest at all in an industry that subjects the farmer to such cruel and destructive economic servitude.

Driven by its desire to reduce the number of independent colonos, the central of the twentieth century has spent whatever capital was necessary to acquire lands and to eliminate any competition, and no law has been proposed to restrain it from this violent course of action, clearly and directly aimed at despoiling the

Cuban colono and farmer. Unhampered and specially privileged, the sugar latifundium has made enormous advances.

According to a table of statistics published in May 1927, by the National Bureau of Statistics with data furnished by the centrales themselves, in 1925–26 the 180-odd sugar mills of Cuba owned over 170,873 caballerías of land (see Table 1). If 134,202 square meters are estimated for each caballería, a total of 22,931 square kilometers is reached—or approximately 20 per cent of Cuban territory. Sugar mills control lands that amount to an area greater than Cuba's third largest province, Santa Clara, which covers 21,411 square kilometers, and greater than the provinces of Pinar del Río and Havana together (21,721 square kilometers).

TABLE 1. *Number of square kilometers and percentage of area in each province owned by sugar mills*

	Square kilometers	*Area owned by mills*
		(per cent)
Pinar del Río	629	5
Havana	1,128	14
Matanzas	2,353	28
Santa Clara	3,718	12
Camagüey	5,846	21
Oriente	9,574	26

Although 185 centrales ground cane, this huge expanse of 22,931 square kilometers is actually in the hands of fewer than 185 proprietors. There are companies that own or control a large number of mills.

This can be demonstrated on the basis of the number of centrales belonging to each company, as cited above by the *Times of Cuba,* and the number of caballerías owned by each central, according to the National Bureau of Statistics. It is revealed that the Cuban American Sugar Company owns six mills with 14,867 caballerías of land; the Cuba Cane Sugar Company, twelve mills with 10,844 caballerías; the General Sugar Company and its subsidiaries, nine mills with 8,972 caballerías; and, finally, to cut short the list, the United Fruit Company, two mills with 8,578 caballerías. These four companies together control twenty-nine mills with 43,261 caballerías, which represent approximately 25 per cent of all the land owned by Cuba's centrales. The latifundium system of property concentration is greater, therefore, than it would appear at first glance from the 185 existing mills.

One central alone may constitute a gigantic latifundium. The Chaparra and the Delicias or San Manuel cover 11,600 caballerías of land; the Cunagua, 9,702; the Manatí, 6,253; the Preston, 5,644; the Jaronú, 4,500; and Mr. Hershey's four mills cover 1,575 caballerías on the outskirts of Havana, which until recently was the province with the highest number of small holdings.

The fact that in Cuba there are vast regions that cannot be farmed, like the Guanahacabibes peninsula, most of the Zapata marshes, the Sierra Maestra, and the mountain massif of Sagua de Támano y Baracoa, gives an idea of the proportion of Cuba's arable land taken over by the sugar latifundia. But in addition to what they own, the mills rent many more thousands of caballerías and, without investing a cent in their purchase, control thousands of farms that are isolated inside the latifundium zone. Since they have no access to public railroads or nearby centrales, these farms are unable to sell their cane elsewhere and are completely at the mercy of the latifundium company. Possibly more than 40 per cent of the total area of Cuba is dominated by the latifundium, and the Cuban farmer living within these huge territories cannot cherish the deepest and most intense aspiration of the man who wishes to provide for his family's future: to own a piece of property on which he can build his home and to cultivate, as a free worker, his own land. On the latifundium property he must live as a feudal colono of the mill, as a laborer or a field hand, and with the advance of the latifundium, less and less Cuban soil remains where he can live independently. Moreover, the independent colono and the local laborer are subject to ruinous competition from the central with its serf colonos and its Haitian field hands.

Part Four

Economic and Social Effects
of the Sugar Latifundium in Cuba

11 The Decline of Economic Independence in Cuba and the Impoverishment of its Rural Population

> Exploitation by the latifundium depends on the availability of a very large proletariat which, separated from land ownership and the other means of production, is converted from a class of small farmers into a mass of day laborers.—*Ferdinand Tönnies,* Desarrollo de la Cuestión Social, *Barcelona, Labor Press, 1927.*

Cuban land originally was allotted, divided, and cultivated by the first Spanish settlers and their descendants.

A thriving community was gradually established, one whose members were deeply attached to the soil they tilled and were better adapted than any other Europeans to the natural and social environment. Mainly rural folk and landowners, they believed in their national identity and fought first for Spain and later for political independence until they became a sovereign state. Cuba existed as a nation from the time the native-born colonists, who far outnumbered the peninsular Spanish residents, divided up and took possession of the island territory and fashioned for themselves an economic life, based on their agricultural activities, distinct from that of Spain. Economic independence was the essential precondition of spiritual and political independence.

The latifundium system is reversing this process. It consolidates thousands of small farms into immense agrarian units; it uproots the farmer from his land; it destroys the rural landowning and independent farming class, backbone of the nation; and finally, it puts an end to national economic independence by converting the society into a mere dependency, a satellite, a workshop, at the service of some foreign power. It reverses the lengthy process which shaped Cuban society and polity and undermines, subverts, and obliterates its national identity. Just as a field is prepared for new farming and different crops by tearing down its fences, abolishing its boundaries, and clearing away its plants and vegetation, so the latifundium is wiping out four centuries of growth in Cuba and is reducing Cuba to an enormous plantation producing sugar for the benefit of foreign consumers.

The sugar latifundium, in addition to attacking the

foundation of Cuba's economic, social, and political structure, must inevitably impoverish the Cuban masses. Economists of all periods and of all schools have recognized that agriculture is the activity most productive and most conducive to real wealth for the general population, much more so than forestry, fishing, and mining, with industry and commerce trailing far behind. For this reason, national welfare depends on how widely land is divided and distributed among the people. When the latifundium deprives the Cuban farmer of his land, it takes away his most effective and often his only means of self-support.

The collective ability of the Cuban to create wealth, to produce, and to increase his properties, is rapidly disappearing. The Cuban capitalist has to live from income or accumulated capital, spending it gradually, and the Cuban daily wage-earner can never hope to own anything more than a little house in some poor section of the city outskirts. The rate of growth of Cuban-held wealth is bound to slow down until it comes to a standstill, and this process, already noticeable, will eventually result in a progressive reduction of national wealth. Like a spring that has dried at its source or wandered from its course, Cuban productive capacity, attacked and destroyed where it originates, is failing little by little. When the money they received for their land is spent, native Cubans will be left paupers in the country where their grandparents owned tobacco fields, pastures, sugar mills, coffee plantations, and estancias, and they will vanish by the thousands into the insatiable maw of the latifundium.

The colono system on company latifundium land is

certain to annihilate the Cuban farming class. The colono, dependent on the sugar mill, can only accept the conditions set for him by the mill or abandon his farm; he has no alternative. And what conditions are laid down by the latifundium company? Knowing the exact production cost, the company makes sure that the colono, working carefully and efficiently, can barely earn a living. Business is business, and it would be ridiculous or stupid—and corporation directors would have to account for it to shareholders—for the company knowingly to grant five arrobas to the colono who can make ends meet on four and a half. Every company calculates down to the last cent the terms under which the farmer will continue to plant cane. Since the colono takes all the risks—drought, fire, carry-over crops, restricted zafra, a fall in price below that expected by the company when it made up the contract—the colono system is ideal for the company, which can never lose.

The colono, in economic bondage, has only one hope: an unforeseen price rise. Such a rise, by introducing a new factor into the year's business, may yield him some profit. Nevertheless, colonos work under such harsh, adverse conditions that almost all of them owe money to the company. Unexpected earnings from a sudden price rise only serve to reduce their debts and encourage them to believe that eventually they will be independent and solvent; so they continue to engage in a ruinous occupation. Against the present diabolical system, colonos have only two possible weapons: association in a union in order to obtain more favorable conditions until that day when the company will be able to do without them entirely and will grow all of its own cane; or government intervention, with a law ensuring a fairer distribution of the industry's profits.[1] Both weapons are dangerous to use and of doubtful efficacy. There is no hope within the latifundium.

In areas where it prevails, the latifundium is creating a society as simple as that of Barbados: high and low employees of the company, and field hands earning a small daily wage, paid by the week. Moreover, employees and field hands have work during only three or four months of the year. Once the grinding period is finished, they have nothing to do, because they have no subsistence plots and there are no occupations except those related to sugar cane. Idle field hands must set out for other parts of the country, which every day becomes poorer and more destitute, to look for some uncertain employment until the next year's zafra.

1. These two suggested measures were put into practice in 1937. The colonos set up the Association of Cuban Colonos, and the government, through the Sugar Coordination Law (1937) and many other provisions, has provided them with protection. [Note to the third edition.]

12 The Increasing Servitude of the Farmer and the Scarcity of Land

The rural exodus constitutes a silent but clearly perceptible criticism of the position of an entire working class. In addition to the fact that they are very badly off economically, they have resigned themselves to a life with no hope of real improvement, since they can hardly keep from feeling enslaved and are frequently deprived of their basic right to organize in defense of their interests.—*Ferdinand Tönnies,* Desarrollo da la Cuestión Social.

The damaging effect of the sugar latifundium on the farmer is not limited to the uprooting of some farmers from the soil by means of large-scale land purchase, thereby swelling the ranks of the city proletariat, and exploiting others by turning them into dependent colonos. Its evil influence can be felt as well, and with increasing intensity, by those who continue to farm their own land, either within latifundium zones or in distant regions.

We have explained that the sugar company does not invest huge sums of money in buying land merely to establish itself as a great landholding enterprise; it does so in order to guarantee that it will be supplied with the cane it needs without having to compete with another central. Once assured of enough cane, it has no immediate need to acquire more land. Therefore, after land is bought to set up a sugar latifundium, two distinct periods may be observed: first, when the company pays as high a price as necessary to secure the number of caballerías required to maintain the sugar mill; and second, when the company, ostensibly indifferent to the properties it is offered, waits to buy them up cheaply at its convenience.

In the first period local landowners, made greedy by the latifundium enterprise, find it hard to resist the temptingly profitable offers they receive; in the second period, those who refused to sell because they expected a rise in the value of their properties, discover that they are just as much under central control as the colonos who work on company land and that their farms have gone down in both rental and sale value. The reason is clear. After the latifundium company has acquired the minimum acreage it needs, it no longer has to buy

cane from the free colono. It then uses its advantage to
decrease the amount of sugar exchanged for every hundred arrobas of his cane and subjects him to the same
harsh conditions as the colono who farms for the sugar
mill. Moreover, large latifundia have their own railway
systems, which exclude the public railway from their
zones of influence and take over all the freight that
might encourage the construction of new lines and public branches. The owner of a farm isolated within the
latifundium's zone of influence finds that the only possible buyer of his cane is the company, which has spread
its tentacles over a radius of several kilometers.

Only an economical and easy means of transportation might make it possible for the independent colono
to break the iron grip of the latifundium. This explains
why it is so difficult to refuse to sell land when a latifundium enterprise with sufficient capital wants to establish itself in a zone. The owner of a farm inside an
area already invaded knows that if he does not accede
at once, his property will go down in value and he will
be liable to disastrous economic bondage. Isolated and
alone, he cannot withstand the latifundium company.
Unless the government comes to his aid and defense, he
has no recourse.

The latifundium not only converts into dependent
fiefs the lands around it, at no cost to itself; it also has
a depressing economic effect on the farmers living in
more remote areas which it has not yet penetrated. The
independent farmer who wants to live freely on his own
land and support his family decently finds that the encroaching latifundium has left very few small and
medium-sized properties, except in lonely, unproductive
regions. Rents are rising, and in order to lease a little

piece of land he is obliged to pay a sizable bonus, a practice long established in certain overcrowded urban areas, but previously unheard of in the country. The scarcity of land for subsistence agriculture (already acute in some parts of Havana province), the need to offer a bonus in order to obtain a subsistence plot, and the steady increase in rents on small properties are terrible burdens inflicted on the farmers by the spreading latifundium. There is hardly a single tenant of small and medium-sized rural properties who can cover his expenses, because of the enormous rents he must pay, the high interest charged on loans and credit, and the lack of an adequate organization to sell his products.

The latifundium is gradually strangling every type of independent farmer, ruining him economically, lowering his standard of living, and making his existence intolerable. It is therefore a powerful agent for impoverishing and urbanizing a people, even in regions it has not occupied, by disrupting the rural economy. The farmer's poverty decreases his purchasing power, and Cuban industry and commerce languish as from a disease that robs the nation of its vitality.

13 The Decline of Commerce and the Restriction of Industrial Development

> If a strict account were made, it would be found that almost all of our commerce is practically bankrupt.—*The general opinion concerning our present commercial situation.*

The economic and social evils that the sugar latifundium brought about in the British West Indies and is bringing about in Cuba are first felt immediately and directly by the independent farming class. In the British West Indies, this class has been replaced by a completely defenseless "colored" population, who work for very low daily wages. In Cuba farmers have undergone a process of proletarianization and impoverishment which, if it is not halted and remedied, will leave them in a situation of parallel economic, social, and political inferiority. But the disastrous consequences of the latifundium system eventually extend far beyond the farmer and affect the whole community. What attacks and destroys one of its vital parts inevitably wrecks the entire social organism. Hence everyone suffers because of the situation brought about by the sugar latifundium —one that has severely damaged commerce, industry, and the public railroads by hindering their development and threatening to restrict further their field of action.

When the agricultural classes are impoverished and their living standards lowered, the purchasing power of roughly 50 per cent of the Cuban population is reduced; this is accompanied by a proportionate decrease in the business volume and, consequently, in the merchandise that is transported by rail. To reduce the purchasing power of the Cuban people is to bring on directly the ruin of Cuba's commerce and industry, which, except for tobacco and cigars, find their market within the country. Consider for a moment that the thousands of Haitian and Jamaican laborers employed in mills consume an insignificant quantity of domestically manufactured products; consider the extent and organization of the latifundium system, which unquestionably reaches perfection in Barbados, and it will be clear that the triumph of the latifundium system marks the end of today's commerce and industry.

In the United States, commerce and industry have developed amazingly, due to a progressively higher wage and income level that has steadily raised the purchasing power of the working class, in the vast majority all over the world. In Cuba, by impoverishing the agricultural class and bringing down wages and by importing cheap labor from the Antilles, the sugar latifundium daily reduces lower-class buying power and effects a gradual stagnation of commercial and industrial activities. And since with less commerce, less industry, and less transport there is also less work in these sectors, the situation of the wage-earning class grows worse, creating the vicious circle in which Cuba has been caught for the last few years. It is certainly to the interest of the sugar companies to try continually to reduce the production cost of sugar; but this can only be accomplished at the expense of the laborer. The cost, then, is that of destroying Cuban rural society and, in addition, wrecking commerce, industry, and the transport enterprises, which depend, for their prosperity, on a population of small landowners and laborers with the highest possible purchasing power.

Our most important commercial cities—Havana, Cárdenas, Cienfuegos, Matanzas, and Sagua—have been suffering for many years from a slow and irremediable decline in all lines of business devoted to supplying the surrounding countryside because, in spite of the constant increase in population, rural consumption is gradually diminishing, especially in those areas where the latifundium is most strongly established. There is no need to forecast—since these events are taking place in full view of any observer—that to the extent that the latifundium economically and socially dominates the country, commercial and industrial activities will decrease.

Ultimately a plantation colony will be formed, dependent for all its activity and life on the sugar industry, just as has occurred in the British West Indies; and Cuba will experience the hopeless decay described by Harlow as the most striking feature of the history of these unhappy islands. The merchants and industrialists can witness today the slow descent of Cuba's agricultural class into a state of economic inferiority, as it is dispossessed little by little of its land and deprived of its principal means of creating wealth, much as highland inhabitants may watch the plains dwellers drown during a flood. The rising tide of the latifundium irresistibly destroys—as demonstrated by the history of twenty prosperous Antillean islands—everything that stands in the way of its final goal: to produce at minimum cost a basic commodity or luxury article for a distant market at a profit, even though that policy will in the long run ruin the producing country economically, socially, and politically.

The sugar latifundium directly affects commerce by driving so-called free trade from its dominions and by making colonos and farmers such poor credit risks that they can no longer trade in the traditional Cuban fashion. Actually, the merchant's best client had been the old sugar mill—not the small one of the first half of last century, but the central prior to 1880—together with the colonos for whom it ground cane. The powerful importing concerns of Havana, Matanzas, Cárdenas, Cienfuegos, Sagua, and other cities made their fortunes by supplying the mill owner and the wealthy colono; the country stores lived off their sales of clothes, foodstuffs, and hardware to the small farmer. The sugar mill did not have enough capital to take over commercial control of its area, and the independent colono bought his provisions wherever and however he liked. In addition, mill lands were limited in extent, and stores of all kinds could be established on nearby properties, from which they could not be driven out.

The great sugar latifundium of today has abundant capital, enabling it not only to get along without the large importing concerns in the cities and the small country stores, but also to exercise authority over them and to claim a share of their profits. It has dispensed with the big business houses, because the sugar companies, with offices in New York or Havana, are organized in such a way that they do not need them. Orders are telephoned or cabled to the United States, except in the case of urgent small purchases; and the American industrialist or merchant has replaced those of Cienfuegos, Cárdenas, and Havana. We shall not dispute the advantages this procedure offers the companies; we simply point out that all sugar mill business is thereby lost to local commerce, which decreases its capital and reduces the number of clerks and workers it can employ.

Moreover, the latifundium company sets up a trading department and a pharmacy, either as its own concern or under a proprietorship to which it gives an exclusive concession within its territory in exchange for a predetermined rent. Small business, therefore, when it exists on the latifundium, must turn over to the latter part of its earnings. The colonos, both dependent and nominally independent, remain; but since the central receives and grinds the cane, it has the colono over a barrel, as the saying goes, and first claim on the payment of his bills. The supply store, in addition, is always liable to suffer heavy losses, because the colono lives in such straitened circumstances that he is perpetually in debt. As a result, to the extent that the farmer has

become a vassal of the latifundium, losing his contractual freedom and his economic independence, commerce has the scope and volume of its business proportionately reduced, together with its earning poten-
tial. The latifundium is taking over all the sources of
wealth, and its economic power becomes daily more
formidable and irresistible. "Today it is my turn, tomorrow it will be yours"—the farmer can say to the
merchant—"the latifundium has the same dismal fate
in store for both of us."

14 Stagnation and the Rising Cost of Railroad Service

> In each region of the different provinces, there are groups who request that a kilometer of highway or a country road be constructed, or that a port be dredged, or a pier built.—
> *General Gerardo Machado, speech given in Santiago de Cuba on June 23, 1926.*

The rapid spread of the latifundium has had an additional negative effect in arresting the development of the public railroads. This has compelled them to keep their rates high and to limit their service, thus working serious harm upon the country. We shall now deal with this last point before going on to the study of measures

we think should be instituted against further development of the latifundium. We are not opposed to the
sugar industry or to foreign capital; we are simply
against a system of agricultural exploitation which will
inevitably ruin Cuba.

The railway made the sugar latifundium possible.
Gigantic centrales such as Delicias, Cunagua, and
Morón could not have existed before the development
of the freight train—rapid, sure, and economical—and
the invention of the cargo truck. Only the railway, and
this is still true after twenty years of extraordinary progress in the automobile industry, could and did give the
central the facilities it needed to extend its zone by many
kilometers. Moreover, thanks to the railway, the central
could be located in the interior of the island at some dis-
tance from loading piers. A glance at a map of Cuba
showing sugar mill locations shows how railroads in-
fluenced the development and location of the mills.

But the public railroad, by permitting the central to
expand its supply area indefinitely, brought it into rivalry with other centrales and obliged it to better the
terms it offered to the colonos. In the cane-growing
zones of the provinces of Havana, Matanzas, and Santa
Clara the centrales competed for possession of *chuchos*
(cane-loading stations) along the railway lines. A single
chucho at the railway loading point meant that the
colono was at the mercy of one sugar mill; when two
or three chuchos competed, the colono was assured of
more sugar for his cane. The public railroad, a factor
in the earlier growth and location of the centrales, gave
the farmer a means of defense. Aware of this, the latifundium companies chose to establish themselves near
the coast, where no public railways exist, and have in-

vested as much capital in the construction of their own railway systems as in the purchase of land.

Through land ownership and control of transportation, the centrales are now in complete command of the situation. Land that has not been bought is isolated within the central and dependent on it for communication with the outside. Centrales owing their origin to the railroads—the Cuban, the Northern, and other lines—have sought to make themselves independent by investing as much capital as necessary to this end. Legislation concerning private railways, dating from General Wood's government and continued under the republic, together with the concession of subpuertos, afforded the sugar latifundium remarkable opportunities to build its own transportation system.

The ownership of railways by the latifundium company has been regarded as legitimate and has been supported by public opinion and the government, because it was thought to be useful to the sugar industry in two ways: lowering production costs by reducing transportation expenses, and avoiding abuses by the railway companies. These two considerations have obscured the fact that the public railway was the principal and almost sole means of defense available to the independent farmer. In its absence, sugar feudalism reigns supreme. The opportunities provided by our legislation on private railways suppressed competition among factories and enabled the sugar companies not only to decrease the amount of sugar received by the colono, but also to subjugate private property within its zone, by monopolizing transportation. The latifundium company was thus provided with a potent instrument of conquest.

But aside from this the sugar latifundium, in its opposition to the public railway that made it possible, has had and will continue increasingly to have a disastrous effect on the country's railway services, unless it is contained. In the first place, it has taken over immense tracts of land in a given region and has constructed its own railway to transport the cane, the sugar, the mill machinery, and all the merchandise imported by the mill and needed by its field hands and employees. These zones are thus deprived of the possibility of a public railroad, which would not have a large enough volume of freight and passengers to cover its expenses, and they are left entirely at the mercy of the latifundium enterprise which controls transportation. Since the construction of the Central Railroad at the beginning of the century, railway development has not progressed as it should. Only one important line, the Northern Railroad, has been added in twenty years; and we all still remember vividly Colonel Tarafa's battle against the sugar companies.

The country has suffered from more than the slowed rate of growth of public railway companies. Today's companies, deprived of an immense volume of freight and passengers by the private lines of the latifundium, have had to live off the rest of the country by maintaining high rates and running their freight trains less frequently. Since their overhead remains roughly the same, they could earn equal or increased dividends by carrying more freight. And by running their freight trains more often, they could offer rapid and economical transportation of domestically produced consumer articles, which would make it more feasible to raise and sell agricultural commodities. The latifundium has not only attacked Cuban society by destroying its vital ele-

ments—rural property and the independent farmer—
but it has had and still has an increasingly harmful and
destructive effect on society's circulatory system, its
public railroads.[1]

1. The construction of the central highway and of feeder roads
has modified this situation, by facilitating transportation by automobile and truck. [Note to the third edition.]

Part Five

The Helplessness of the Latifundium
Against Foreign Competitors

15 The Futile Struggle of the Cuban Sugar Latifundium Against the Social and Economic Organization of the United States

A principle which has gained much popular approval as a satisfactory solution of tariff problems is that of equalizing costs of production. This principle is now embodied in law. Under section 315 of the Act of 1922 the President is authorized to change the rate provided in ¶ 501, in case the rate there provided does not equalize costs of production between the United States and its chief foreign competitor [Cuba, in the case of sugar],

to such an extent that the new rate will equalize such costs of production. The Tariff
Commission is entrusted with the task of
securing the necessary cost data.—*Philip G.
Wright, Sugar in Relation to the Tariff, In-
stitute of Economics, established by The
Carnegie Corporation of New York, 1924.*

The sugar latifundium company carries on its battle to
strengthen its position and increase its profits on three
different fronts: against sugar production in the United
States and its island possessions (Hawaii, Puerto Rico,
and the Philippines), against sugar production in other
countries, and against the Cuban farmer and laborer.
On this last, domestic, front it has achieved absolute
superiority. We will try here to describe its futile and
destructive struggle against an invulnerable rival, the
North American sugar industry. The Cuban latifundium company's adversary is not, strictly speaking, a
special branch of North American production; rather,
it is the total economic and social organization of the
United States, a formidable instrument for expansion
and for national defense, conceived and created through
the combined efforts of its industrial magnates, statesmen, and workers. We are moved to study such a fruit-
less and unequal battle not out of idle intellectual curi-
osity but out of concern with the effects of a silent economic war on the Cuban people, whose ruin will follow
on the destruction of the national sugar industry.

On the United States front, the sugar latifundium is
in direct conflict with the beet sugar producers of the
Western states and the cane sugar producers of Louisiana, Puerto Rico, Hawaii, and the Philippines; and it

competes indirectly with all the sugars from other sources that reach the North American market. Since sugar is a commodity that hardly varies in quality, the struggle is based on a single factor—price. And the Cuban industry has recourse to only one weapon—the reduction of production costs. This is the basis for the continued existence of the latifundium and the sacred banner in the name of which all Cuba is supposed to make any sacrifice demanded of it. In order to lower production costs, Cuba is expected to allow the un-limited concentration of rural property in the hands of a few companies, less numerous but more powerful every year; to facilitate the company railway and the subpuerto; to permit the importation of cheap labor which depresses local wages; and to accept without argument the fact that the colono will lose his economic independence and will receive less and less sugar for his cane. At the same time, so as not to blunt the only weapon available to the industry at present, the Cuban people are expected to put the welfare of the latifun-dium company before their own destiny and autonomy.

Lowering production costs, the only weapon the in-dustry possesses and the one to which it entrusts the de-fense of Cuba's interests, is completely ineffectual, be-cause the North American economic organization has another weapon that automatically nullifies Cuba's: the raising of its tariff.[1] Every cent saved in production costs, at the expense of the Cuban laborer's redoubled efforts and standard of living, is canceled by the cent that is thereupon added to the North American tariff.

1. When this measure did not suffice, the United States instituted the sugar quota system in 1934, reserving a limited quota for Cuba. [Note to the third edition.]

The enemy is invulnerable and the latifundium owners know it. But since the Cuban people are the ones to suffer the consequences, the owners beguile themselves, or they beguile the people, by encouraging the vain hope that the United States will, for Cuba's sake, renounce the system and industrial methods that have made it so incredibly prosperous. This attitude is either very naive or very disingenuous.

The United States, with a population of 120 million scattered over an immense territory abounding in natural resources and free from customs barriers, has developed industrial production on a scale never before known to humanity. Although North American industrial genius, initiative, enterprise, and energy have been very important factors, historians, economists, and statesmen agree that the unlimited consumption capacity of its vast domestic market has been essential to the magnificent development of its production. North American industry has tried to realize its aims as fully as possible: (1) by establishing large industrial plants in order to reduce manufacturing costs; (2) by standardizing its products and by mass production, which permit extensive mechanization and reduce the number of laborers employed; (3) by specializing its labor and paying it the highest wages in the world; (4) by giving the working class through higher pay a share in the increasing productivity; and (5) by recovering from them, through their consumer expenditures, the greater part of their wages. The Ford plant whose employees and laborers travel to work by the thousands in Ford automobiles is a typical example.

This marvelous system, which steadily raises the living standard of the whole nation, and especially of the working class, can operate when production for domestic consumption takes place in a virtually closed economy, as in the United States. The laborer, like the capitalist, is interested in increased and cheaper production, which brings within his means a lower-priced article, formerly only enjoyed by the rich. At the same time, the steady rise in the population's purchasing power guarantees ever-increasing profits to the industrialist. Therefore, this system, which embodies a brilliant concept of *national* progress, is supported by the statesmen in Washington, by industry, and by the American Federation of Labor, representing the working class.

North American economic and social organization, the basis of its extraordinary prosperity, can be thrown out of balance in only two ways: by the immigration of foreign labor that would compete with the American for factory jobs and force down wages or by imports of foreign goods manufactured by cheaper labor that could profitably compete with domestic products in the local market. Against these two dangers, statesmen, capitalists, and the working class together have erected two formidable and absolutely effective barriers, immigration laws and customs tariffs, which have eliminated any threat from abroad.

The system might appear to harm the consumer, but since the main consumer is the laborer himself—who is not primarily concerned with saving money, as is the European laborer, but with earning better wages in order to raise his living standard—the immense majority uphold an organization that ensures national prosperity, widespread employment, and high wages. In addition, the tariffs are carefully formulated, taking into account the production costs of imported articles, and precisely adjusted to each case. When consumption can be satisfied wholly out of domestic production, the tariff is absolutely prohibitive; but when North American output cannot meet all the demand, the tariff is fixed at a minimum that will allow all domestic production to be sold before importing any cheaper foreign merchandise; meanwhile, every effort is made to find a substitute for the imported article in question.

This is the case with sugar. The United States tariff makes sugar production in North American territory invulnerable against Cuban or any other foreign competition, and guarantees that the domestic article will be sold first. If our latifundium enterprise, by exploiting the colono or the laborer or by improving agricultural and manufacturing methods, could offer sugar at a reduced price in the New York market, the tariff would automatically be raised to re-establish the former price. The Fordney-MacCumber sugar tariff and the United States Tariff Commission, together with the President's legal authority to increase or lower the tariff by 50 per cent without consulting Congress, serve precisely this purpose.

When, during this century, Cuba managed to reduce production costs by obtaining higher yields, opening up new farm lands, giving less sugar in payment to the colono, and importing cheap labor from the other islands, all our savings disappeared in United States customs houses. In order to sell sugar in New York, additional duties had to be paid in exactly the same amount as production costs had been lowered. The North American producer and his workers suffered no loss; neither did the North American consumer. As

Mr. Coolidge, advised by Mr. Hoover, had foreseen, the price of sugar did not go up; and the United States Government profited by becoming the principal beneficiary of Cuba's industry, collecting at its ports of entry all that was saved in Cuba. The only losers were the Cuban people, who worked more and earned less.

At present, the government of the United States, without investing a cent in the sugar business in Cuba, receives an annual income of more than 140 million pesos by permitting the sale of Cuban sugar in its country. This sum is almost double the total annual revenues of the government of Cuba. If tomorrow, by putting the farmer and laborer on half rations, we should succeed in taking a cent off production costs, we would shortly see a tariff rise of that same cent.[2] North American sugar interests would not suffer and the consumer would be unaffected, because the market price of sugar would not change; the government in Washington would charge 200 instead of 140 million pesos for the privilege of selling Cuban sugar in the United States; and probably the latifundium companies would continue to earn the same dividends. But those who would receive 60 million pesos less for identical work would be the Cuban farmer and laborer.

Some Cubans entertain the hope that, for the sake of Cuba, the United States will abandon the social and economic policy that has made it a great nation. Such

2. This prediction was soon to be fulfilled. In 1929 Cuba did not enforce measures to restrict sugar production and harvested a crop of more than five million tons. The price of sugar in New York fell from 3.37 cents a pound in 1927 to an average of 1.72. The North Americans reacted by quickly approving the Smoot-Hawley law, which raised the tariff against Cuba from 1.76 to 2 cents a pound. See the Epilogue to this book. [Note to the second edition.]

a hope could be realized, under present conditions, only if the interests of the American people were directed from Washington not by statesmen and businessmen but rather by idiots or imbeciles. Doesn't this mean that Cuba should change its system?[3]

3. The Roosevelt administration, without essentially modifying the protection provided the domestic sugar industry, in 1934 began a new policy of tariff reduction and of allocating to Cuba part of the United States market. [Note to the third edition.]

16 The Inexorable Evolution of the Latifundium: Overproduction, Economic Dependence, and Growing Poverty in Cuba

[The system] cannot work steadily. It must always go by fits and starts. It is like a steam engine without a regulator. . . . Off goes every productive machine in the country. Everybody is piling his goods onto the market with a reckless disregard for the morrow. . . . There is no effort made to ascertain where the balance between supply and demand is fixed. The result is a choking of the market, depression in trade, unemployment, financial loss and bankruptcy.—*J. Ramsay Mac-Donald,* The Socialist Movement (*New York, Holt, 1911*), *p. 72*

We have seen that the sugar latifundium company wages a futile price war against North American sugar production, and that the latter is made invulnerable by being able to manipulate the United States tariff. Anyone not deliberately blinded to the facts will see that the present system results in the annual transfer of about 140 million Cuban pesos to the United States, which, without having to invest a cent in the sugar business, drains into its customs houses nearly 50 per cent of the gross value of all the sugar Cuba manufactures.[1] We have also pointed out that experienced businessmen demonstrate an extraordinary naïveté and ignorance of human psychology when they expect the United States to change its carefully worked-out system, the basis of its prosperity and entirely to its advantage, simply to enable Cuba's sugar companies to earn back all that it would give up thereby.

To complete this exposition of the evils of the latifundium, it remains only to explain how the Cuban sugar manufacturers' obsession with lowered production costs will inevitably complete the latifundium cycle

1. The Smoot-Hawley tariff, which imposed an even higher tax, was approved in 1930; and in June 1932, Cuban sugar was sold in New York at 2.57 cents a pound, of which 2 cents went to the customs, and 0.57 went to the Cuban producer to cover all his expenses. [Note to the second edition.] The situation has improved for Cuba since the institution of the new United States sugar policy that is referred to in footnote 3, Chapter 15. [Note to the third edition.]

and, as in the other Antilles, convert Cuba into a poverty-ridden country, devoted entirely to the production of sugar, and completely dependent—economically, socially, and politically—on an export market.

Lowering of production costs is the procedure normally employed by the industrialist to earn a profit, when he cannot force up the price. In the case of a product for domestic consumption, the economy as a whole is always benefited, especially if it is a basic commodity, because the cheaper article is placed within reach of the local consumer. However, if it is an export product, lowering production costs is useless unless it serves to overcome foreign competition; otherwise, the consumer in other countries simply pays less money for the labor that produced the article. Only when competition forces us should we resort to the desperate expedient of lowering production costs, in effect thereby earning less money for our labor.

If the sales price did not change, lowered production costs could result in a gain for the whole society, if distributed equitably among the central, the colono, and the laborer; but the history of the price of all consumer goods sold in a competitive market shows that any reduction in cost is always reflected in a lower sales price, since whoever reduces costs is prepared to utilize part of his profit margin to increase his sales volume by selling his product more cheaply than that of his competitor. Over the last century, sugar prices have declined every year in value, in absolute or relative terms, compared with the steady rise in the cost of living for almost all civilized peoples. Prices have gone up when wars or other such events have disturbed the normal balance of production; but they have soon resumed their downward trend. This trend, together with the advantage derived from a reduction in overhead expenses, is the most powerful and constant incentive to large-scale production which, by stimulating consumption, increases the volume of business. To produce more at less cost is the desideratum of modern industry.

All of this is commonplace and easy; we are dealing with simple and familiar economic facts. But when we come to an agricultural industry such as Cuban sugar production, which is based on extensive cultivation of an "export crop," the facts take on an ominous cast. More sugar at less cost means that a greater proportion of our national territory will be devoted to raising a single crop; it means lower wages for the Cuban laborer, without any benefit to the Cuban consumer, who lives on imported articles, not on sugar.

With declining prices, the central is compelled to produce and sell more sugar every year, because only in that way can it show a profit. Otherwise, invested capital would earn lower dividends or none at all. The latifundium is relentlessly forced to continue growing, to expand, to improve its machinery in order to extract more sugar, and to acquire more terrain until it has devoured all the country's arable land. This has happened throughout the Antilles; under the present system it is happening in Cuba in full view of anyone who cares to see. The constant expansion of the latifundium, driven by inescapable economic forces, cannot help but extend monoculture and will consequently leave less land, capital, and labor for other productive activities. The more Cuba comes to depend on sugar cane, the less possibility there is that it will ever be able to diversify its agriculture and supply its population with consumer goods. Cuba's economic dependence will increase and we shall be completely and hopelessly at the mercy of the sugar buyers and of foreign governments. The day that Cuba finally becomes one huge cane plantation, the republic and its sovereignty will vanish; and we are embarked on this course.

Just as the company tries to maintain its dividends by manufacturing more sugar in order to compensate for the lower price per bag, so the farmer and the laborer try to plant a larger crop and to have more cane ground in order to maintain their annual earnings by working additional days at lower wages. Hence, not only the company, but also the workers, advocate an expanding industry, because their lower wages make it imperative that they work longer hours. "More sugar, more sugar!" urges the latifundium company. "More sugar, more sugar!" the laborer also shouts, though both are being crushed ruthlessly between the rollers of a giant grinding mill. But more sugar results in overproduction, which depresses the market and lowers the company's dividends and the worker's wages, and both must cry out again: "More sugar, more sugar!" Cuba is caught in this vicious circle. Meanwhile, the latifundium spreads, defended by the selfishness of those who are concerned only with how to maintain profits and by the intellectual shortsightedness of those who look only at one small part of the picture, instead of at the whole panorama.

Cuba is going through the same experiences and the same stages as the British West Indies, whose culture and social progress have been enthralled until now by a dreadful system of land exploitation. When this system is introduced into a national economy, it can only be neutralized by wise, forward-looking, and firm measures. Cuba has taken some action, thanks to Necessity, that harsh, implacable teacher whose lessons are always learned *a posteriori*. In the last two years, the government has imposed a limit on the zafra and has prohibited the clearing of new lands for cane cultivation. These are the first steps toward curbing the evil, the recognition of the existence of a danger that only the state can combat. If the zafra had not been restricted by the government, the companies—driven by those forces that compel them to produce more and more—would have sent to market more than five million tons of sugar, thereby intensifying further the fall in prices caused by overproduction. The zafra has been reduced and, consequently, the farmer and the laborer have had less work, less income, more poverty.

But we should not look for the remedy within the vicious circle of the latifundium system itself. More sugar at less cost will sooner or later turn Cuba into a new Barbados. We have nothing to say to those who accept that fate for their country and are satisfied with the present situation. We do have a message for those who love Cuba in another way: all their intelligence, resolution, and faith should be used to solve this tremendous problem and to ensure the economic independence of their country. The latifundium, which has stained history with suffering and misery, which brought about the downfall of Rome, which has led to innumerable wars and revolutions, which has produced the decline of the Antilles, is now slowly and relentlessly strangling the Cuban people.

Part Six

A Program of National Action
Against the Latifundium

17 The Decline of the Republic

> When we achieved the political independence
> of our country, we fulfilled a great obligation.
> Now we have another duty. We must direct
> labor in such a way as to ensure the economic
> independence of the Cuban worker. Only the
> latter independence will guarantee the for-
> mer. What was won through bloodshed must
> be made to endure.—*Enrique José Varona,*
> De la Colonia a la República (*Havana, Edi-*
> *torial Cuba Contemporánea, 1919*).

There is no doubt that the sugar latifundium has been
the cause of the decay of all the Caribbean except those
islands that continued under Spanish rule until the nineteenth century. The Cuban of today must fight against

becoming an economic serf of the latifundium, just as he battled yesterday against political subjugation by the colonial system. It is imperative that an enlightened national program of action be drawn up, adopted, and put into effect as quickly and energetically as possible. This can be accomplished if the gravity of the problem is understood by the executive and legislative branches of the government; by Cuban public opinion—meaning the people who think and feel as the founders of our nation thought and felt—and by all Cubans or foreigners who are moved by a natural affection for the country where they have established their moral and material interests and who are concerned with protecting those interests. The moment has arrived when we cannot afford to hesitate or take half measures. Either we resign ourselves to the increasing economic bondage to which we have been condemned by the latifundium system or we decide to summon up all our intellectual and spiritual resources to check its progress and counteract its effects.

But for Cuba's sake, action against the latifundium must not take the form of action against the sugar industry, or against domestic or foreign capital. The sugar industry has been, still is, and may continue to be a source of wealth and progress in the nation. The capital that promotes, organizes, and develops the industry is essential to production; without it, the country would be plunged into misery. Nor do we decry the latifundium merely in a spirit of contentiousness or in a fit of passion. In a business like the manufacture of locomotives or shoes, growth is restricted to extension of the plant over a few more acres, and the effects of overproduction of locomotives or shoes are felt only by the capital invested in those activities. If this were the case of the sugar latifundium, our sole concern would be to help it, at least insofar as the problems of our producers affect the general welfare of the community. Having warned it of the dangers inherent to its policy, we would probably then wait for the law of supply and demand to take over and prevent it from going beyond reasonable limits, by lowering the profits of capital invested in such an enterprise.

If the latifundium company grew vertically, in the manner of a giant skyscraper, instead of horizontally, we would probably have nothing to say about its development. Instead of insatiably swallowing up new lands in order to continue the traditional practice of extensive agriculture and using its landownership to dominate the farmer, the latifundium company should try to increase production by means of intensive agriculture, as many companies are now doing of their own accord. It should try to control mosaic disease, the moth borer, root-eating grubs, and other pests and diseases of sugar cane, which cause widespread damage to the fields; to apply fertilizer over broad areas; to breed varieties of high-yield cane; and to establish irrigation systems wherever possible, employing capital now dedicated to the purchase of lands and to the construction of costly railway lines, sometimes sixty or seventy kilometers long, to link those lands to the sugar mill.

The latifundium company should also try to develop the zones it has taken over, dividing its land into lots and promoting colonies of farmers who would have permanent economic ties with the sugar mill; and it should make available to the farmer its vast mechanical resources for those operations that require expensive

agricultural machinery. If the latifundium company
would replace its ruthless methods of commercial exploitation, handed down from past centuries, by just
and reasonable methods in keeping with the political
and economic advancement of recent years, we would
have nothing to say against it. On the contrary, we
would argue in favor of a capitalism that developed and
constructed, instead of clinging to the old system of
merciless despoilment.

To repeat—we are not attacking the sugar industry
or foreign capital. We are combating a system of land
exploitation that has been widely censured in the name
of justice, social order, and humanity. It is a system
that has brought misery to one of the most extensive,
fertile, and beautiful archipelagoes in the world. It has
turned the people into bitter, poverty-stricken multi-
tudes who, if no attempt is made to remedy the errors
and crimes of the past, may kindle tomorrow the same
dreadful social conflicts that have devastated and still
ravage the Old World. Our crusade against such no-
torious evils is not inspired by a narrow nationalism,
but by ideals of justice and civilization which aim at
achieving the collective good through two basic means:
(1) maintaining a strong, stable national economy and
realizing a fair distribution of the products of labor
among all classes; and (2) establishing foreign trade
relations that are not based on our position as a dependent producer of raw materials, sentenced to work
more cheaply every day for a consumer nation that
raises its living standard at the expense of the country
it dominates.

The latifundium must be fought out of love for Cuba,
which rightfully expects its people, institutions, and

civilization to endure, and out of an understandable self-interest in defense of all that has been created here by the labor of Cubans, Spaniards, and others. The bitter resentment of today's Negro peasant in Barbados against his latifundium exploiter—described by Harlow —is spreading over all the Caribbean. When the almost nine million men of different races and origins who populate the islands reach the exploding point, there will be a social holocaust comparable to the one that left opulent Haiti in ashes and has kept it on the fringes of civilization for more than 130 years.

But since the latifundium is now as powerful as the country, it cannot be opposed without help from the state. In the hands of an intelligent and active people, political institutions are society's most effective means of defense. A government achieved at the cost of Cuban lives must work to recover the right of Cubans to till their own lands as independent farmers. The country must use its authority and laws to defend the people who created it and who depend on it for their welfare and their existence. In the silence of the swelling expanse of sugar cane fields, glistening green under a tropical sun, a harsh and decisive test is being prepared for our institutions. If the Cuban government does not act promptly, it will have revealed within and without its utter inadequacy. It will indeed have failed hopelessly, because by not sustaining the ideals of the Cuban people, it will discredit our revolutionaries of the past century who forged those ideals out of their tears and blood.

18 Bases for a Program of Action Against the Latifundium

It was recognized that unless a better understanding of living conditions in the open
country was obtained, our civilization would
become lopsided and would deteriorate. It
has been found that the country is not self-
sufficing and inherently able to progress
without conscious social effort; and that the
welfare of the nation depends upon the
maintenance of a rural civilization.—*Paul L.
Vogt,* Introduction to Rural Sociology (*New
York, Appleton, 1920*).

National action against the development of the latifundium has to be both cautious and determined, it has

to follow an over-all plan, and it has to be based on knowledge of the causes that facilitated and encouraged the growth of latifundium exploitation. Its immediate aim must be to check that growth, but it should also have a wider purpose for the future: to create a healthy, strong economic organization that will immunize Cuba against the virus of this agricultural plague. The success of Cuba in its defensive measures against the economic forces that drag it toward decay will constitute a new experience in this field of human activity. E. M. Miller, of the New York National Bank of Commerce, has analyzed the enormous damage done to our country by its one-crop sugar economy, the primary consequence of latifundium exploitation of agriculture. In his excellent documented article recently published in *Commerce Monthly* and reprinted in the Havana newspaper *El Mundo,* on July 6, 1927, he states:

> There is as yet practically no experience on which to base a judgment as to the probable course of economic evolution in tropical countries with nationally conscious populations whose standards of life and outlook are derived from those of the Temperate Zone.

Mr. Miller is correct when he speaks of tropical countries. All of them, and especially the Antilles, have been colonial plantations without a national consciousness, lacking any patterns for living besides that afforded by the brutal exploitation of a destitute working class for the benefit of the financial interests of distant metropolises. Cuba is perhaps the first tropical country with a national awareness and with evolved patterns for living to be confronted with this problem. This is why Mr. Miller is also right when he says at the end of his article:

> Cuban experience during the next few years ought to afford much light on the probable course of economic events in many other tropical areas now being developed. Exploitation can hardly be more than a passing phase of the awakening now in progress in the Torrid Zone.

The process of exploitation, which in Mr. Miller's opinion cannot be more than a passing phase, has already lasted more than three centuries in the Antilles. Since the beginning of the century, its development in Cuba has been headlong. Let us pray that the national conscience and standards of life and outlook derived from the Temperate Zone, which Mr. Miller attributes to us, will spare our nation—through a supreme effort of intelligence, will, and patriotism—from the common unhappy fate of the Antillean countries.

In any action against the latifundium, all rights and interests established under the laws of the country must be scrupulously respected. The latifundium is a blight on the economy, but lack of respect for a legally constituted right, even if that right is the result of a mistaken government policy, does still more harm to the country, both at home and abroad. We shall have to work methodically, with wisdom and perseverance, to free ourselves from the burden of our past errors. Fortunately, the Cuban people are better off today than were the slaves of Antigua in 1833 who, two days after their liberation by plantation owners (who had already taken over all the arable land of the island), found themselves subjected to an even harsher economic slavery, which they have not since been able to shake off. We are rather in the position of the freedmen of Jamaica in 1838, described in Chapter 3: we still own enough land to dig in and defend ourselves. If we keep it in our possession, divided among our farmers, we can escape our impending "manifest destiny"—not the traditional one of annexation, but that which has befallen Barbados, Antigua, and Jamaica.

Moreover, we have another hope in the fact that the sugar latifundium of our times resembles the statue dreamed of by Nebuchadnezzar in the Bible. As interpreted by the prophet Daniel, the statue's head was of gold, his breast and arms of silver, his belly and thighs of brass, and his feet partly iron and partly clay. A stone cut out of the mountain struck the statue on its feet and destroyed them, whereupon he was reduced to dust. The tireless scientific research that has long been carried on in the United States may at any moment result in a discovery that will reduce the sugar latifundium to dust.

A program of action against the latifundium, designed to create a sound economy that will ensure the increasing welfare of the Cuban people, should consist of three basic points, each of which has its own purpose and covers a series of problems that may appear secondary, but are very important: (1) no further expansion of the latifundium, (2) no further importation of cheap labor, and (3) land of his own for the farmer. The first point is aimed at preventing further concentration of landed property in the hands of a few Cuban or foreign corporations organized exclusively for profit. The second point is aimed at improving the wages of the laborers who farm the cane and work in the zafra, by following the policy that has had such magnificent results in the United States. The third point proposes to keep Cuban territory in the hands of the Cuban people, and to have as much land as possible subdivided and cultivated by a class of small farm owners, who would constitute the basis not only of a prosperous agriculture but of a stable society.

No further expansion of the latifundium. Drastic measures should be promptly enacted, which would prohibit absolutely any future concentration of more than a given number of caballerías—whether by purchase, lease, or any other procedure—in the hands of a single entity or company. There is nothing new about this kind of legislation. It has been successfully adopted in all countries where the state has provided for the defense of the rural population against the feudal type of latifundium exploitation. It has helped Denmark achieve one of the most progressive and flourishing agricultures in the world. The Philippines, under United States rule, have enjoyed this protection for some time, but Colonel Thompson, President Coolidge's special envoy to the Philippines, has suggested that such protection be ended in order to promote immense rubber plantations. This might benefit the large North American companies that manufacture automobile tires, but certainly not the Philippine people, whose farmers are safeguarded by that law. A legal limitation upon the amount of land that may be owned by one person or company should be absolute and should apply both to Cubans and to foreigners. It would not be a political measure directed against foreigners, but an economic measure to limit the latifundium.

No further importation of cheap labor. This measure may hurt vested interests if it is suddenly enforced. It therefore calls for a more detailed discussion (see Chapter 20). To bar new labor imports is probably the most effective way to limit the zafra and to avoid overproduction. If the industry's sudden and sharp development, far beyond the resources of Cuban capital and labor, had not been made possible by foreign financial power in search of profits and dividends, there might have been no overproduction. If permitted uncontrolled importation of cheap labor—whether white, Negro, or Oriental —the latifundium enterprise will turn more and more to administration farming, the elimination of the colono, the appropriation of lands, overproduction, and the steady reduction of the wages and living standard of the Cuban rural laborer.

Land of his own for the farmer. Cuba should draw up a careful program to promote the creation of small and medium-sized properties, similar to that which has been followed since 1899 in Denmark with brilliant results. This program should be based on the allocation of a large share of the annual budget to a loan program that facilitates the purchase of farmland and requires the construction of a house with specified hygienic facilities. These loans should be made only to workers with families who can prove that they have lived several years in the countryside and that they intend to go on living there and engaging in agriculture. The loan would be secured by the property and would be repaid in easy installments over twenty-five or thirty years. Starting with a minimum of two million pesos a year, an insignificant amount in our budget, and using loan repayments to set up a revolving fund, in twenty years Cuba would have invested fifty million pesos in providing the most responsible and enterprising sector of our rural population with its own farmland. Attached in this way to the soil, thousands of families would be emancipated from the harsh exploitation to which they are now subjected, and their living standard would be raised; most important of all, our economic organization would be strengthened, and Cuban land kept in the hands of the Cubans who cultivate it.

No further expansion of the latifundium; no further importation of braceros to force down the wages of the Cuban worker; land of his own for the farmer: these are the essential points of our program, which is not opposed to the sugar industry, capitalism, or foreigners. It is a formula for defending our community and safeguarding the rural working class of our country, composed for the most part of native Cubans, white and Negro. It purports to ensure social justice.

19   Security for the Sugar Industry
      and Protection for the Colono

The sugar problem has been under discussion
for some time. When sugar sells for a high
price, everyone is satisfied and no one fore-
sees that its price may fall later. It is indispensable that provisions be made promptly for
such a contingency. Mill owners fear government interference in their affairs, and colonos
do not believe any good would come of it.
Nevertheless, I believe that intervention, like
any other matter that may affect the country,
should be studied by the government.—*General Gerardo Machado, speech given in San-
tiago de Cuba on June 23, 1926.*

Land appropriation by the latifundium enterprise answers the industry's need to protect itself against any possible shortage of raw material which would jeopardize its capital investment. In this respect, the company only obeys the law of industrial concentration which is to control all means essential to business and large-scale production. Our motto, which should become law, is *no further expansion of the latifundium.* But the kind of evil we are combating must be attacked at its roots. The sugar companies are compelled to invest huge sums of money in acquiring limitless land; the interest accrued on this investment is added to the cost of production, and the industry depends on financing by banks that come to support and dominate it completely.

As long as the motives for the growth of the latifundium are not counteracted, laws prohibiting concentration of landownership will be inefficacious because they will ruin the centrales. And yet Cuba must put an end to the destruction of its small properties. We therefore feel that a solution must be found to assure the existence and prosperity of sugar companies, using whatever means may be necessary as long as they are not harmful to the colono or the country.

Capital invested in each sugar mill must be protected and competition among companies—not only in the purchase of cane, but in the purchase and rental of lands —must be eliminated. For this purpose, four fundamental measures should be adopted:

1. No new centrales should be established in Cuba, unless authorized, and only if they are located outside the zone of present mills and meet requirements set forth by the law.

2. Each sugar mill zone should have its limits defined,

wherever possible, and laws should be enacted to provide facilities for industrial concentration and convenient distribution of sugar mills throughout the country.

3. The government should aid the central to develop intensive agriculture on lands adjacent to the mill and to reduce capital invested in field areas used exclusively for cane agriculture (often kept fallow) and in the central's private railway system, which would decrease expenses and, accordingly, production costs.

4. The number of arrobas of sugar to be paid the colono for each hundred arrobas of cane should be standardized for the whole country or for certain regions, and it should be revised every three or four years by taking into account average costs of agriculture and manufacturing; this figure would be specified by a national commission made up of representatives of centrales, colonos, and the government.[1]

The first measure is in defense of capital invested in the sugar business, regardless of whether it is Cuban or foreign. In view of the present world situation with regard to sugar, that capital is now in danger, and it can only be further jeopardized by the policy all countries are following, of encouraging only national industry and backing tariff protectionism.[2] Cuba, therefore, has less

---

1. The Sugar Coordination Law (1937) has solved this problem by allotting to the colono a fixed percentage of the sugar processed by the mill. [Note to the third edition.]

2. This prediction was soon fulfilled. A world glut of sugar and the Smoot-Hawley tariff, which acted as a strong stimulus to sugar production in the United States and its territories—Puerto Rico, Hawaii, and the Philippines—reduced the price of sugar and restricted the sale of Cuban sugar in the United States. As a consequence, Cuba was plunged into a terrible and unprecedented crisis. [Note to the second edition.]

interest in promoting new sugar mills and opening up new areas of cane agriculture than in defending the industry that already exists. In order to fight steadily mounting foreign competition, measures should be taken to free the sugar industry from internal danger and from the useless expenditures made necessary by competition among centrales.

The demarcation of a zone for each sugar mill would improve the organization of the industry on a national scale. In some regions there is a surplus of sugar mills, many founded before the War of Independence or during the First World War period of high prices. This situation makes it difficult to concentrate industry, and the existence in these regions of sugar mills large enough to operate as real centrales results in a loss of labor and capital that is added to production costs. Ideally, there would be a minimum of large sugar mills, to be located where they would best serve the country. We advocate not the small mill, the old-time *cachimbo,* but the great modern factory, set up where it will be most useful. Such an organization of the industry offers obvious economic advantages; less overhead, less absorption of capital in small mills, less investment in lands that are sometimes unproductive, and less money spent on railways and transport. It entails only one risk: conversion of the central into a monopoly. If that risk can be avoided, the industry and the country as a whole will be greatly benefited by the elimination of needless expense, and we shall be fortified for our struggle against foreign competitors.

Actually, these zones of influence already exist in many areas where the most powerful companies, realizing that their competition was both costly and destructive, divided up the territory and agreed not to invade each other's jurisdiction, thereby forcing colonos and farmers to sell their cane to a single mill. What is now a private conspiracy should be made a public law that would protect capital invested in sugar mills without exploiting the colono.

There are several ways in which the government can help develop intensive agriculture in lands adjacent to each central and increase the yield per caballería of cane and sugar: lowered taxes; lowered import duties on fertilizer and on raw materials and machinery for their processing; support of company research on cane diseases; breeding programs to produce high-yield cane; new farming techniques and mechanization of field operations; state irrigation projects and subsidies specified by law for companies that carry out their own projects, etc. The purpose of this aid would be to maintain the present volume of output or, if justified by future demand, to increase it. At the same time, it would reduce the area of national territory devoted to sugar cane agriculture, and would conserve a great deal of the unproductive capital now invested in land, private railways, and transport expenses. It would make more land available to other forms of national production, counteracting the dangers of monoculture and freeing Cuba from its increasing dependence on foreign markets. And the sugar industry itself would derive incalculable advantages from an economy strengthened in this manner.

Finally, as suggested, the amount of sugar to be given colonos for every hundred arrobas of cane should be standardized, either for the whole country or for regions. This would not only eliminate rivalry between sugar companies that invade each other's territories by railway, but would also safeguard the colono.

At present, land and communications are owned by sugar companies dominated or entirely managed by banks, which, owing to inadequate farm credit legislation, make no direct loans to colonos. As a result, not only colonos who work on sugar company fields but the so-called "independents" of the western provinces are reduced to economic vassalage. The importation of laborers paves the way for administration farming which, as it spreads, supplants the colono, and will finally return Cuba to an agricultural system essentially no different from that of slavery times before 1868, when the colono neither existed nor was necessary. Restriction of the zafra would mean that their cane will be left in the field; and the more independent they are, the more the farmers will suffer, for the mill naturally tends to grind its own cane or the crops of farmers most in debt to them. Lack of restriction of the zafra would contribute to overproduction, lowered prices, and their ruin.

What course should be followed? Unless the government comes to their assistance with all the powerful resources at its disposal, the farmers will have no alternative but to accept the will of their mighty adversary and sink gradually into despair and poverty. They can escape this unhappy fate if they are legally guaranteed a reasonable financial reward, tied to the percentage of sugar in their cane, which the government can set according to average farming and processing costs. Once the existence of present mills is assured, the territorial expansion of the latifundium contained, the just and legitimate rights of the colonos upheld, an industry—free from the problems of internal rivalries and needless capital expenditure—will be in a much better position to face its foreign competitors.

20 No Further Importation of Foreign Laborers

The second of our proposals for a program of national action against the latifundium, *no further importation of foreign laborers,* is not new in the history of Cuba. In the course of more than fifty years this traffic was denounced by José Antonio Saco; Dr. Antonio Gonzáles de Mendoza, founder of the Association to Oppose the Purchase of *Bozales* [freshly imported African slaves], introduced into Cuba after 1865; the Cuban commissioners to the Board of Information in 1866; the Yara revolutionaries; and, finally, the Liberal Party, founded after the Treaty of Zanjón. Cuba's finest citizens fought against the importation of contraband bozales and the tyranny of slave traders, and for their country's sake risked exile, property confiscation, imprisonment, and death. The Cuban ideal ultimately triumphed, thanks to the heroism and sacrifices of the Ten Years' War and to the determination of the Independence leaders. Not only was slavery totally abolished, but so, too, was the importation of contracted Chinese labor. In the forty years thereafter, Cuba continued to produce sugar, in spite of all the gloomy predictions of the advocates of slavery.

The colono system was created and production came to be based on more humane and just practices. The United States Military Government, under General Leonard Wood, enacted a farsighted law that closed Cuba's door, apparently forever, to so-called undesirable immigration—not of a given race, but of foreign workers of any nationality who would force down the wages of native Cuban workers and in effect thereby lower the general living standard of the Cuban people. But history repeats itself, and man's selfishness and avarice, once aroused, can never be restrained; it leads individuals and societies to commit the most dangerous errors. For almost sixty years, from 1821 when Spain was supposed to have abolished the slave trade until the end of the Ten Years' War, Cuba's highest interests and every spiritual and temporal law were violated by the importers of degraded labor, who used the same argument now advanced by the importers of Caribbean workers: "If the importation of cheap labor is prohibited, the sugar wealth of Cuba will be destroyed."

At that time a contraband trade was maintained through the conspiracy of all who were so venal that they closed their eyes to the harm done their country:

the slave dealer, a power in the colony and usually a colonel in the *Voluntarios*[1]; the administrative officials, from the captain general who received as much as an ounce or an ounce and a half of gold per bozal down to the lowest lieutenants who were paid insignificant sums; and the mill owner, unless he was an exceptionally honorable person, such as Aldama, Juan Poey, or Antonio Gonzáles de Mendoza.

The slave trade was hypocritically defended on grounds of "national integrity" and loyalty to Spain. Oh sugar, sugar—we might say in a parody of Mme. Roland's words—what crimes have been committed in thy name! Those who fought the trade were severely punished for threatening the sugar wealth of the island; while those who profited from it would rejoice if they were alive today, feeling themselves exonerated.

In order to rationalize the contraband trade in bozales, from 1821 to 1880 it was maintained that climate prevented the white worker from engaging in the labors of sugar cultivation or milling. Only Africans— it was said—could endure such heavy labor, or rather, not endure it, since a shocking percentage of them died. But considerations of justice or humanity had no place in this reasoning. The worker, the human being, as the Count of Pozos Dulces said, "was also transformed into raw material and became part of export production."

The Cuban public always recognized that the fundamental question was not one of race or climate, but simply of economics. *Low wages* were the objective.

1. The *Voluntarios* were a semimilitary group organized by Spain and open exclusively to white men; they were led by a council of colonels.

The Cuban commissioners wrote to the Board of Information in 1866:

> The truth is that in Cuba there is not a single person with any knowledge of the history of our sugar production who is unaware of the real significance of the constant outcry for more labor, or who anticipates any decline in Cuba's agricultural output if it should no longer receive the influx of laborers that are annually poured into its fields by clandestine trade and Oriental immigration. No, it is not an agricultural reverse that is dreaded and forecast in the dark warnings also reflected in this Report. Some fear loss of the profits they make, more or less legitimately, from these immigrations; others fear loss of the swift returns they get on their financing and brokerage of contracts drawn up for the clearing and plowing of new land. There are those who realize that, in the absence of cheap or forced labor, they will have to attend to their estates much more closely and see to it that they are well managed; and there are those who resent being deprived of the opportunity to recoup a fortune they did not create or make secure under more favorable circumstances.

These words are as valid now as they were in 1866. And they are borne out by the fact that from 1880 to well into the twentieth century when the first permits to import Haitians and Jamaicans were granted, after the republic was established, the sugar industry continued to progress without importing cheap foreign labor. But toward the end of 1912, authorized by a decree handed down by President General José M. Gómez, the United

Fruit Company imported 1,400 Haitian laborers. During the two terms of President General Mario G. Menocal, from May 1913 to May 1921, 81,000 Haitians and 75,000 Jamaicans entered Cuba, according to figures compiled by Carlos M. Trelles. The 1925 report on immigration and passenger movement, published by the Statistical Section of the Ministry of Finance, gives data on immigration into Cuba, which is presented in Table 2. Of the immigrants who entered Cuba during

TABLE 2. *Number of Haitians and Jamaicans immigrating into Cuba, 1921–25*

	Haitians	Jamaicans
1921	12,483	12,469
1922	639	4,455
1923	11,088	4,455
1924	21,013	5,086
1925	18,750	4,747

the 1921–25 period, 72,165 were illiterate. All of these foreign laborers were imported by sugar companies. The net effect was to depress the wages of native Cuban workers. And yet, even at present, in the four provinces of Santa Clara, Matanzas, Havana, and Pinar del Río, only local workers are employed by the industry. In Camagüey and Oriente, where Cuban labor is also available, laborers are imported because they cost less. If the importation of laborers were absolutely prohibited, local labor could harvest all the cane, but it would have to be paid higher wages. Although this is not to the advantage of the sugar companies, it is vitally important to Cuba's

domestic economy and to the Cuban worker. A laborer
from the first four provinces will never go to Camagüey
or Oriente to earn, for a three or four months' zafra, a
miserable wage that does not even cover his railway
fare. But he will go if he is paid a good wage and assured of employment over a reasonable period. Oriente
and Camagüey will also be avoided by the crop farmer,
the colono, and by any foreign immigrant with ambition,
no matter of what origin, because in those provinces
laborers are not offered land and they are badly paid.

Land and high wages are the two main incentives that
attract ambitious, enterprising immigrants. In Camagüey and Oriente, the latifundium monopolizes land and
pays poor wages. How can these provinces ever hope to
be populated other than by unfortunates fleeing the poverty of their own countries? Sometimes it is argued that
the daily wage there is the same as in the rest of the
island. Of course it is; the wage of the rural worker in
Cuba descends to the same level as the wage paid the
Jamaican migrant worker. If centrales in other parts of
the country could not find labor willing to accept the
Jamaican wage level, they would also import foreign
workers. Precisely for this reason, we have maintained
that labor importation not only means less employment
opportunity for the local worker, but it also depresses
his wages and lowers the living standard and purchasing
power of all of Cuba's working class.

Plans are being made to promote the immigration of
peasants into the sugar cane regions of Camagüey and
Oriente. We ask those who honestly support these ideas:
Do you believe that unless the immigrant from abroad
or from the western part of the island is offered land and
steady, well-paid work, he will be attracted to the lati-

fundium fields? To contend that the present system can encourage immigration is either to mock the sincerity and candor of the people, or to demonstrate a naïveté bordering on idiocy. Why do no English immigrants go to the British West Indies, British Guiana, or British Honduras, while there are thousands who emigrate to Canada, South Africa, and New Zealand? Because in the former countries there is no land available and wages are so low that the worker has no hope of bettering himself, whereas in the latter countries he is offered a chance for land of his own, high wages, and unlimited possibilities of success and prosperity. Cuba can have no illusions about this matter. Either it seeks to continue as a cultured and progressive nation or it resigns itself to the future of a plantation colony, denying its past, its present, and its ideals. Barbados or Canada? If Cuba aspires to be like the latter, it must close its doors to contracted cheap labor, the mainstay of the latifundium.

But is it possible to do without the importation of cheap labor from the Antilles or elsewhere? The small colono does not need them. The larger colono of Camagüey and Oriente at present depends on them because, under the terms of his contracts with the companies, he receives much less sugar than the colono of the western provinces and he can stay in business only by underpaying his labor. The sugar companies can undoubtedly dispense with foreign workers; if the centrales between La Trocha and Havana give seven or more arrobas of sugar and still prosper, the centrales east of La Trocha —which are more modern and better equipped, have a higher extraction rate and less transportation expense, and which only give five or five and a half arrobas of sugar to the colonos—can well afford to reduce their dividends or to economize in their administrative and other expenses so that they can pay somewhat higher wages to labor. The large colono cannot get along without imported labor and offer better wages unless he obtains more favorable terms in his contracts with the companies. Until this problem is solved these colonos will be allied with the latifundium companies and, therefore, against the interests of Cuba and the Cuban workers. They will even harm themselves, because importation of Antillean labor leads directly to administration farming and elimination of the colono, whom the latifundium tolerates as a useless, costly intermediary, to be gotten rid of as soon as possible.

Vested interests were the greatest obstacle to the abolition of slavery. They stand in the way of any effort to make progress, to establish social justice, to defend the fundamental interests—also vested—of Cuba's national integrity and economy. Mistakes in economics, as in anything else, are paid for in this life, and capitalism was very much in error when, blinded by greed, it suddenly created an industry in underpopulated regions and carried them to their ruin in a wild production race. The sugar industry maintains an obviously untenable situation because it is faced with the necessity of a complete readjustment, which it dares not and probably cannot make alone. It is now evident, and has been for the last two years, that we must restrict not just an occasional zafra, but production generally, so that it will more nearly equal demand. Sacrifices must be made, and by those producers who operate on credit and who cannot continue to exist without the importation of foreign labor. It is an outrage against justice that while millions and millions of arrobas of cane, planted and cultivated by native-born Cubans, are left standing in the fields because zafra restrictions prevent their being milled, foreign laborers are imported to harvest most of what is ground by certain mills. If there must be restrictions, they should be on labor performed by the imported worker.

21 Land of His Own for the Farmer

> The war of 1868 and later the war of 1895
> were not primarily fought to break our politi-
> cal ties with the mother country, but to trans-
> form Cuba from a colony into a nation.—
> *General Gerardo Machado, speech given in*
> *Santiago de Cuba on June 24, 1924.*

Of the three basic points that we have proposed for the
program of action against the latifundium, two are negative in character: no further concentration of land in
the hands of a few; no further importation of cheap
labor. But it is not enough to check the evil. It is necessary to counteract its effect and promote the creation of
a large class of farmers, progressive and debt-free, who
will till their own soil and cement the foundations of our
society. This leads us to our third point.

All the agrarian and economic objectives of the republic—diversification of crops, restriction of output to

the level of demand, reinforcement of the sugar industry against foreign competition, development of the industry in all its sectors, advancement of commerce, rapid increase in population, steady rise in the standard of living, higher government revenue, a domestic economy that will make the nation economically independent—in a word, the welfare and progress of Cuba, depend on the adoption and application of a wise and patriotic policy of land distribution. Agriculture is the activity that most effectively creates community wealth and only an agriculture based on the independent farmer insures constant land improvement and the existence of a strong, progressive, and stable rural class.

Edouard Herriot summed it up admirably: "The earth requires one's actual presence." This is the meaning of the ancient Greek myth. When Heracles wrestled with Antaeus, giant son of Poseidon and Earth, he found that each time he threw him to the ground, Antaeus rose again with his strength renewed from touching his mother Earth. In their struggle against the latifundium, the Cuban people are like Antaeus. If they are secure in the possession of the land, they shall be invincible. If the latifundium succeeds in separating them from it, they shall be doomed. By returning to the earth they shall regenerate themselves; otherwise, they shall perish. Even independence did not subject Cuban resources to so severe a test. In spite of the harshness of the colonial system, when the people owned and tilled their own soil, they could forge their national identity and later win independence. A country that is politically unfree, but that possesses and cultivates its own lands, can win its freedom, as Cuba did. But a free people who relinquish their land to another have taken the path to economic servitude and social and political decay. Within a quarter of a century, either the latifundium or the republic will no longer exist. The Cuban people will have land and independence, or they will have lost them both. That, not annexation, is Cuba's manifest destiny in the twentieth century.

The promotion of a large class of independent farmers, even inside the latifundium zones, would be the mainstay of a stable sugar industry. Under pressure of world competition, the latifundium resorts to reducing production costs by cutting wages. But this strategy cannot be carried beyond certain limits. Europe, the United States, and all other sugar-producing countries are increasing their output. In this struggle some must be destroyed and others will survive. Cuba's natural advantages are neutralized and counteracted by the protective tariffs of its rivals. Countries with strong economic organization will triumph. But the latifundium system is weak and vulnerable; it lives by exploitation, and is not upheld by a large class of farmers who have their future assured by a rich and varied agriculture. Without mounting foreign competition, the sugar latifundium could continue indefinitely, but its opponents are entrenched behind tariff walls, and the latifundium has no battleships or armies to use against those walls. Unless it avails itself of its natural ally, the farmer, it will be heading for collapse and ruin.

There is only one desperate hope: that the latifundium enterprise realizes that its defense lies in uniting its interests with those of the Cuban people. Otherwise it will be annihilated by its rivals. If it did not have Haitians and Jamaicans at its disposal, it would already be arranging reasonable terms for Cuban countrymen to plant its cane, instead of treating them with scorn and arrogance. The latifundium has tyrannized the colono but has itself become a slave of the bank, and it cannot survive without the foreign laborer. Because it still does not dare ask the government directly for permits to import laborers, it supports the large colono, who performs this function for it.

The Cuban sugar industry would be much stronger and more resistant if each central could count on an adequate supply of cane, grown in the mill zone by hundreds or thousands of small colonos, owning their farms and sure of having their basic needs met by a diversified economy. They would then be able to help the mill overcome foreign competition not only by accepting less than cost price for their cane for one year but, if necessary, they could survive two or three zafras without collecting a cent. The latifundium position based on credit financing that can be withdrawn from abroad at any moment is, in spite of its apparent solidity, very vulnerable. A Cuban agricultural and landed class would offer much sturdier resistance. If the sugar companies were not forgetful, they would remember that they were saved at the time of the 1920–21 bank crash by farmers and laborers who, in an admirable demonstration of sacrifice and collective discipline, agreed to work during the zafra season without pay, for only their meals. At that time they were congratulated and praised. They were later forgotten; but this surely indicates who are the natural and indomitable allies of capital invested in the sugar business.[1]

1. In the crucial years since 1927 these facts have been confirmed. In the western provinces, many small mills with independent colonos have withstood the disaster, while powerful North American

If the sugar companies, instead of monopolizing land and eliminating the independent colono, would subdivide their land and make it available to farmers on easy terms payable in cane, and then help them raise not only the cane but also food crops, every mill would become the center of a nucleus of hard-working colonos who would have their present and future prosperity bound up with that of the company. Any loss suffered by the central in the execution of this policy certainly would be compensated for by the higher value of its land, owing to the region's increased population and business activity. This task cannot be accomplished overnight, but it should be undertaken immediately by the companies in order to protect their own interests. The Cuban government, strongly backed by public opinion, can and should give every assistance to enterprises that begin to replace their old methods of maximum exploitation with fairer practices.

Sugar companies, in their own interest and as an elementary means of defense against competition from abroad, ought to replace latifundium exploitation with the creation and promotion of farm colonies in their zones. The Cuban government, after arresting the development of the latifundium by prohibiting further importation of braceros, is no less obligated to come to the assistance of the colono by making it possible for him to purchase farm land.

It is urgent, we repeat, to initiate the distribution of public lands among rural families, following the proce-

---

sugar companies, in spite of their Haitian labor, have been ruined. Finally realizing this, the industry has united with the colonos. [Note to the third edition.]

dure employed by Spain to establish solid foundations for government and society. In addition, the state should create a national fund to promote small rural property similar to the special fund for public works, that would enable the farmer to purchase property and build a house with certain standards of comfort and hygiene by means of a loan secured by the property.

As long as Cubans own and till most of the land, Cuban society will be a vigorous reality, capable of maintaining and perpetuating itself no matter what setbacks and harsh trials fate may reserve for it. The Cuban people should sink their roots firmly into Cuban soil, from which they will derive energy and life. Only the earth can give the country the vital force needed to resist the powerful agents that are relentlessly undermining our national integrity. If the land is lost, all shall have been lost, including liberty and honor.

Epilogue

This book's main thesis—that if the sugar latifundium is permitted to develop freely it will inevitably lead to the economic ruin and the social and political decay of the country where it flourishes—has unfortunately been further substantiated in Cuba from 1927 to the present [1934]. Cuba's prolonged economic crisis is unparalleled in the island's history; the political and social unrest and the moral and material confusion of Cuban society have no precedent. If Cuba does not act promptly and energetically to resolve its problems, it will fall still farther behind the march of civilization. Once the relentless process of Antillean decay reaches its fatal conclusion, not only will the Cuban people suffer, but the country will have to renounce its role as a center of

Added to the original text in the second edition, published in 1934.

social, agricultural, industrial, and scientific progress for the rest of the Caribbean.

Let us recapitulate a few facts. In 1927 the Cuban sugar industry fought on three different fronts: one abroad, to overcome its foreign competitors; and two at home, to restrain the internecine rivalry of its centrales and to dominate colonos and exploit workers.

Sugar-producing countries everywhere continued their struggle to control the market and eliminate their rivals by producing the greatest possible amount of sugar at the lowest possible cost. The resulting overproduction and immense sugar surpluses on the world market rapidly depressed prices. Countries that needed to supplement their domestic output found that the low price of imported sugar constituted a threat to their industries. They immediately raised protective tariffs, which stimulated internal production and curtailed the free market. The free market steadily grew smaller, and overproduction increased; as the sugar war between large countries continued without interruption, prices kept falling.

In this difficult situation Cuba, which together with the Dutch colony of Java is the world's largest producer of sugar for export, initiated a policy to restrict its output. This policy had two purposes: first, to raise the price of sugar in the United States market where, thanks to the Reciprocity Treaty of 1902, it had supplanted all full-duty sugar purchased by that country; second, to induce other countries to follow the same policy of restriction, in order to reduce world surpluses and to achieve a balance between supply and demand.

There were serious internal and external obstacles to this policy of restriction. In Cuba the position and interests of all the sugar companies and all the colonos did not necessarily coincide. Some time ago, certain North American sugar-refining companies, which buy most of the raw sugar milled in Cuba, had decided that it would be convenient to establish or purchase centrales on the island. The great trust, the American Sugar Refining Company, owns among others the two large and modern centrales, Cunagua and Jaronú, in the province of Camagüey. The Hershey Company, in addition to being a refinery, owns several mills in the province of Havana which supply sugar to its chocolate factories in the United States. The powerful United Fruit Company, with banana and other business interests in Central and South America, also owns large centrales in Cuba which supply sugar to its own buyers in the United States. Moreover, there are many other centrales which, through their connections with huge trusts in the United States—manufacturers of soft drinks, candies, and other articles that require sugar—are always certain of selling their product.

Centrales of this type were naturally opposed to restriction; they had their own markets and nothing would induce them to restrict their output. The main business of the American Sugar Refining Company is to refine, not to produce, sugar; it obtains a larger profit margin between the raw sugar that it buys by the thousands of tons and the tariff-protected refined sugar that it sells to the North American market where raw sugar is not used, except in certain industries. As the price of sugar goes down, it not only raises the profits of the refining company, but provides it with a pretext for paying lower wages to the employees and laborers of its Cuban mills. If sugar is kept cheap, the Hershey Company will make more money on its enormous sales of chocolate, cocoa, and cookies, and it will have to pay less in Cuba to its workers (though in fairness to Mr. Hershey, we must say that he has always offered the highest wages).

Other centrales, similarly connected with industrial enterprises, are in the same situation. The trust as a whole derives profits from an industrial product of which sugar is only an ingredient; therefore, the lower the price of sugar, the higher the profits of the entire producers' combine. These facts must be recognized and borne in mind in order to understand the apparently illogical opposition of powerful companies to any attempt to reduce the production of their mills in Cuba and to raise the price of sugar.

In addition to centrales in this special position, there were others that sold in the free market but were much stronger for various reasons—they had more capital, more fertile land, better location, more modern machinery, a Haitian labor force, etc.—than the rest of the centrales that were also obliged to sell in a competitive market. The stronger central owners realized that Cuba would have to reduce its output, but they thought that this should be accomplished by eliminating the weakest mills. Three or four zafras at ruinous prices would bankrupt the most vulnerable centrales, and restriction would come about naturally by the simple law of survival of the fittest.

Against these two groups who opposed restriction (although each for a different reason) were arrayed all the other mills that were facing ruin from overproduction and low prices. They hoped that restriction—their last resort—would deliver them from a sorry plight.

Colonos were divided along the same lines as the centrales. Colonos who worked for the mills that were owned by refineries and companies with a guaranteed market for their sugar in the United States were opposed to restriction for the same reason as their employers. Even if they had to accept a low price, they were sure of selling their cane. Faced with the alternative of planting less and leaving part of their cane in the field in the hope of a better price later on or selling all their cane immediately at a sacrifice, they did not hesitate to choose the latter.

The situation of the great majority of the colonos was more serious. Restriction would cause them considerable hardship at the beginning, but they realized that overproduction and low prices would soon bring about their total ruin. Only the imminence of disaster drove them in desperation to accept restriction, but they were always ready to be convinced that they might be saved without it.

There remained the great mass of laborers, whose wage rates varied as did the market value of sugar, lagging behind when prices rose and descending rapidly when they fell. In either case the laborer was the loser. With overproduction, he would obtain a few more days of employment a year, but at a miserable wage that sometimes would not even cover his keep; with restriction, he would earn somewhat better pay, but would work fewer days.

The government had to take a position concerning this conflict of interests. Like the majority of mill owners, it favored restriction at the beginning of the economic crisis, in spite of strong protests from opponents of restriction. Cubans and Spaniards who had lived in Cuba for generations owned most of the weak sugar mills, which not only ground the cane of the largest number of colonos but employed native Cubans as laborers. Liquidation of these mills would be a catastrophe for the most heavily populated provinces of Cuba and would cause the bankruptcy of numerous *ayuntamientos* (municipal governments), which receive their principal revenue from centrales located in their respective regions. Moreover, at that time it was thought that the crisis would soon be over, and therefore all sugar mills should be protected. Restriction was aimed at giving national protection to the majority of mills and Cuban colonos, and it became an official policy through a law of Congress. But even after restriction the crop was much larger than could be sold on the United States market where Cuba enjoyed tariff preference, and such enormous quantities of sugar flowed into New York that its price there fell lower than in London and Hamburg. For this reason it became necessary to limit the amount of sugar to be exported to the United States; but under-capitalized centrales in financial straits kept the price below normal by continued sales.

In order to deal with this problem, an agency was organized to become the "single seller" of the sugar crop. This plan could not be successfully applied because it was inadequately financed, and later it was replaced by a very complicated system of export quotas for sugar sold in the U.S. market. Using as a base the total amount of cane ground by each mill, the reduced amount was to be prorated first among the centrales and then among the colonos of each central, so that all would share in the loss. But this necessitated taking a census of all cane grown in Cuba and such a census, even if carried out with the utmost impartiality and good intentions, was bound to involve frequent errors and injustices. Taking place as it did in the midst of a terrible crisis and in spite of angry protests against restriction, it gave rise to violent accusations and complaints by those who felt themselves victimized by favoritism.

Cuba's effort at restriction, so difficult and so unpopular, helped somewhat to check the fall of prices, but nonetheless it was not favorably received in other sugar-producing countries. Since Java, the only large exporter of sugar in the Far East, had no trade rivals in India, China, and other nearby countries, it maintained a higher price on these markets than on those of Hamburg, London, and New York. Any sugar not disposed of in its exclusive markets was dumped in Europe to supplant Cuban sugar and that of its other competitors. Java therefore had no interest in entering into restriction agreements. Other sugar-producing countries took advantage of Cuba's restriction in order to sell their sugar at higher prices and enlarge their industries.

After a two-year trial, during which it steadily produced less sugar and lost ground in its markets, Cuba's situation was critical. In view of the mounting poverty and despair, the sacrifice it had made by restriction appeared to be worse than useless. Opponents of restriction and advocates of a "free zafra" won support and put pressure on the government to abandon its restriction policy and the artificial controls it had placed on the industry, and to permit free operation of natural laws. They wanted an open war of sugar interests, not only in Cuba but on the international scene, which would adjust supply to demand by eliminating the weakest mills.

As a result of the battle, they foresaw that production would be restricted to the survivors, certain to include refinery centrales and others in privileged positions.

A fundamental objection was raised to the free zafra. Maximum production and the lifting of all controls on export to the United States meant a declaration of war on the North American sugar industry. The United States would accept the challenge and defend itself by raising its tariff. This measure would not only nullify the Cuban effort, but the additional protection would stimulate sugar production in North America's own territory, Puerto Rico, Hawaii, and the Philippines. Cuba, without gaining any advantage, would run the risk of losing its only sure market and bringing on the total ruin of its industry. The supporters of a free zafra replied that the United States government and Congress, in the interest of the North American consumer, would not enact new tariff increases. Cuba could triumph over the North American industry and win the entire market. The Cuban government acceded to the pressure of the general public and in 1929 granted a free zafra without any artificial controls. With the 1929–30 zafra added to crops carried over from previous years, Cuba put on the market the largest zafra in its history: 5,156,000 tons.

The effect on world price was instantaneous and calamitous. Facing ruin, North American sugar producers asked the United States government and Congress to intervene. The Smoot-Hawley tariff was approved without delay, raising the duty on Cuban sugar from 1.76 to 2 cents a pound and turning over to North American customs an even higher percentage of Cuba's diminished sugar income. But this was not all. Under the protection of increased tariffs, the beet-growing states of the West and Louisiana, Puerto Rico, Hawaii, and the Philippines were encouraged to produce more sugar. Cuba, with declining prices, began to lose rapidly the only valuable market it could depend on. It should be noted that the privileged centrales that had opposed restriction and brought about the change in Cuba's sugar policy were not damaged by the Smoot-Hawley tariff. Their production was guaranteed by their outlets, and the higher tariff actually improved the competitive position of articles manufactured in the United States with their sugar. Moreover, they produced at full capacity in Cuba, paying very low wages adjusted to the low price of sugar on the world market.

After the fiasco of 1929–30, most of the centrales and colonos were aware that they were headed toward a catastrophe. The restriction policy again gained support, and by this time Java and other sugar-producing countries were gravely concerned. One more free zafra in Cuba could have disastrous consequences for the world market. A European conference was planned by the main sugar-exporting countries, in order to reach an agreement on new international restrictions. To make possible restriction and a world accord, Cuba had to approve the "Chadbourne plan," named after the North American lawyer primarily responsible for it.

The plan which emerged for world regulation of the sugar industry had two objectives: first, each contracting party agreed to gradual restriction of its production to the extent recommended; second, each contracting party agreed to keep a given percentage of its stored surplus off the market, in order to raise sugar prices. This surplus sugar would be sold over successive years in amounts to be determined by progressively reduced production. It was hoped that by the end of five years world output would balance consumption, surpluses would be disposed of, and prices would be high.

In Cuba it had been customary for mills to pledge their sugar surpluses as security for credit extended them by banks. It was therefore necessary to enlist the cooperation of banks, so that they would not place such surpluses on the market as the term of each pledge expired. This problem was solved by creating an official corporation made up of sugar producers which took over all pledged sugar surpluses on condition that they would be sold gradually under the rules of the plan. In exchange for the sugar, banks were given bonds, issued by the Cuban government, to be amortized annually out of income from sale of surpluses. When all the surplus sugar had been sold, if the bonds were still not amortized, they would be redeemed by means of a tax paid by all the centrales. Once the banks were satisfied that they would not suffer any loss, they gave their consent. This was essentially the famous and much-discussed Chadbourne plan.

This plan signified a new restriction to maintain price stability, a new limitation on the amount of sugar that could be exported to the United States and to Europe and, consequently, a new apportioning of export and production quotas among centrales and colonos. The application of these measures inevitably created endless complications, errors, injustices, abuses, and grievances. Cuba became a cauldron of conflicting interests—social, economic, and even political—boiling over with the hatred engendered by poverty, suffering, greed, ambition, and oppression.

The Chadbourne plan could not save Cuba, no matter how beneficial its effect on world production and market, because it did not include the North American economy. The latter, protected by the new and higher Smoot-Hawley tariff, continued to increase its output and to reduce Cuba's preferential share of the market. The Cuban sugar crisis became worse and the country fell into the direst extremities. The yearly averages of the price of sugar in New York from 1927 to 1933 tell the whole story of the Cuban calamity. In January 1929, raw sugar was at 3.37 cents a pound, after payment of duties, but it averaged only 2.95 for the year; 2.45 for 1928; 2.99 for 1929; 1.47 for 1930; 1.34 for 1931; and 0.93 for 1932. Its price at the beginning of 1933 was 0.66 cents a pound; and it reached its lowest point the first week of June 1933, when it sold for 0.57 cents a pound.

It must be remembered that at the same time that prices were falling, Cuba had to reduce its zafras and limit its sales to the United States, whose market was increasingly supplied by domestic production and was protected and stimulated by the Smoot-Hawley tariff. Machado's government tried to relieve the crisis by establishing a protective tariff and by negotiating trade treaties with Spain, France, Italy, and other countries. New industries were created, and Cuba began to supply most of its basic commodities. But before these measures could have any positive effect and just as the price of sugar started to improve, the Machado government, besieged by a strong and determined revolutionary movement, was overthrown through intervention of the United States Ambassador Sumner Welles, following instructions from his government.

Since the fall of Machado on August 12, 1933, the three revolutionary governments that succeeded him have made no essential changes in the sugar policy. The Chadbourne plan is still in effect, as is restriction of the zafra and limitation of exports to the United States and Europe. Export quotas for these markets are still apportioned among sugar mills, and production quotas are assigned to each central and each colono. The Machado government deliberately favored small centrales, largely in the hands of Cubans and Spaniards, in its distribution of production quotas, and this practice has been continued. In the same spirit of nationalism, the revolutionary governments have also adopted measures to protect the laborer and the colono. On the other hand, the so-called undesirable immigration—mainly of Haitian laborers—has not been entirely prohibited and the latifundium remains unchallenged.

The most recent event of importance to the sugar industry has been the replacement of the Reciprocity Treaty of 1902 by a new trade treaty with the United States, signed in August 1934 by the provisional revolutionary government of Colonel Mendieta. President Roosevelt's government made an estimate of the United States' annual consumption of sugar and allotted market quotas to its continental producers and insular possessions. It also reserved a share of its market for Cuba: 1,920,000 short tons at a reduced tariff. Besides this important benefit, the new treaty granted preferential treatment to Cuban rum, tobacco, and certain fruits and vegetables during seasons when these articles were not being produced by United States farmers. In exchange for these concessions, Cuba had to make tariff reductions that consigned practically all of its import trade to the United States.

The problem of the latifundium is by no means solved in Cuba. With the treaty, the United States has temporarily alleviated the Cuban crisis and has saved from total ruin for the moment most of the North American capital invested in the Cuban sugar business—possibly 70 to 80 per cent of all sugar capital. But actually the latifundium problem remains unchanged and Cuba, now economically more dependent than ever on the fluctuations of the United States trade policy, is less free to expand its trade with the rest of the world. The Cuban government must take advantage of the respite afforded by the treaty to draw up and apply measures to protect and strengthen the national economy.

Appendix 1.
Recent Evolution of the
Sugar Industry

by José Antonio Guerra y Debén

That sector of the public concerned with social conditions but out of touch with recent developments in the
sugar industry believes that the economic and social
problems involved in the manufacture of sugar continue to be those which existed in Cuba prior to 1929.
This judgment, correct twelve or fifteen years ago, is no
longer valid.

Not that these problems have been entirely solved, or
that the present organization of the principal source of
wealth provides the Cuban people with everything Cuba

This appendix was added to the third edition, published in 1942.

considers necessary to justify the existence of any industry. Although there has been some progress, Cuba is still far from that goal.

The problems have not disappeared, but they have changed in appearance and character and, basically, they are now different from those prevailing in the 1920s, when the sugar industry was criticized in such works as the first edition of *Sugar and Society in the Caribbean* and *La Agonía Antillana*. The revolutionary upheaval of 1933, which has failed to achieve not only the essential aspirations of the most progressive and enlightened groups but even the modest and immediate aim of giving Cuban workers a decent living standard, nonetheless had a profound effect on certain aspects of the economic structure, especially on the sugar industry.

Since independence, Cuba has been faced with a grave problem, which became increasingly severe after the 1914–18 conflict. The accelerated and relentless advance of the sugar latifundium threatened to drown Cuba in a flood of sugar cane and to convert it into a typical plantation colony, farmed by cheap labor imported from other Caribbean islands. This unchecked trend to monoculture had resulted in an unstable economy dependent on the fluctuating price of a single commodity. Moreover, in Cuba as elsewhere, the development of the sugar latifundium inevitably had other serious consequences. The independent farmer was gradually eliminated as the latifundium literally tore him away from his land, ground him between the mill rollers, and discarded him as useless waste material.

In addition, the labor force in sugar factories and cane fields was displaced by low-paid workers imported from Jamaica and Haiti. With a lower living standard, they took over almost the only benefit derived from the latifundium—the wages it paid for the exhausting labor of field hands and factory workers. As its final effect on the country's domestic economic structure, the headlong growth of the sugar latifundium was an insurmountable barrier to the development of other industries and branches of agriculture. It was therefore impossible to establish gradually a more balanced national economy, where production for internal consumption would not be constantly and fruitlessly sacrificed to a swollen export trade in an underpriced article.

By the 1920s the sugar latifundium was so powerful that no government measures, however determined or extreme, could have kept it from continuing to absorb land. And this assumes that the latifundium would not have used its influence to prevent such measures from being adopted. It must be remembered that, since becoming a republic, Cuba had failed to heed the warnings and advice of some of its finest citizens, who had tried to persuade the government to exercise the most elementary precautions to protect Cuba's autonomy against this threat.

Fortunately, by one of those tragic paradoxes so frequent in the history of Cuba, the world economic crisis that erupted in the autumn of 1929, with immediate repercussions in Cuba, came just in time to save the situation. The same economic forces that had encouraged the latifundium process now acted to check it, if not to reverse it.

The sudden collapse in the price of sugar and the drastic reduction in exports between 1930 and 1933 brought about profound social disturbances. However, it also accomplished by itself what united national effort might not have been able to achieve: it swiftly paralyzed latifundium expansion and thereby made possible the elimination of the evils arising from a single-crop economy. The industry's excessive growth was halted because exports failed and sugar prices dropped. Both of these causes were wholly economic and beyond the control of the sugar corporations that operated in Cuba.

It is possible to gain an idea of the extent and strength of these factors by noting that sugar production fell from 5,156,284 tons in 1929 to 1,995,079 in 1933, a reduction of 61 per cent in four years' time. During that same period, Cuba's exports to the United States dropped from 3,643,121 tons in 1929 to 1,396,119 in 1933, which means that its share of the American market decreased from 52 to 25 per cent. Its exports to the world market were similarly affected.

With such a reduction in exports and the lowest price level in history (0.57 cents a pound), the sugar latifundium had no further incentive to expand. The low prices it had obtained by exploiting the Caribbean laborer and enslaving the colono no longer enabled it to overcome tariff barriers and win markets.

At first glance, it might appear that since the sugar latifundium's paralysis was caused by purely temporary circumstances, it continues to be a menace. We would like to note some of the facts that persuade us to the contrary. The sugar crisis was world-wide and the result of overproduction. In addition to the development of sugar production in new areas, there was an increase in the output of areas that produced sugar before the war. It is unlikely, therefore, that conditions will ever again create new demand on such a scale that latifundium expansion would be unleashed anew.

This seems especially to be the case since sugar companies own or control more than enough land in Cuba now to double present output without further displacement of the farmer. The present zafra of almost four million tons of sugar and molasses was produced from about 60,000 caballerías of cane; the area possessed or dominated by sugar mills extends over some 240,000 caballerías, which means that only a fourth of the available land was actually utilized. Moreover, modern mill machinery, new cane varieties, and improved agricultural methods have raised industrial yields appreciably.

There is still another factor which, although not economic, is no less worthy of consideration. Leaders of the sugar industry in Cuba, as in other countries, appear to have profited by the experience that culminated in the 1933 catastrophe. They have learned that while the latifundium may be all-powerful in Cuba in its relations with farmers and workers, it is helpless before the tariff measures and market regulations imposed by the consumer countries protecting their domestic production. They realize that the only way the industry can be sure to survive is through international agreements that replace cut-throat competition with some degree of control and cooperation, which in turn will make it possible to establish better conditions for sugar workers.

This new approach to international sugar policy has been adopted by the governments of the principal exporting countries. For the most part, the sugar industry has cooperated in an effort to stabilize the industry by adjusting supply to demand and obtaining prices that will be both reasonable for the consumer and profitable for the producer. The United States, which under Hoover had followed an ultraprotectionist policy that almost bankrupted the sugar industry, inaugurated a quota system in 1934. Although Cuba has not recovered its former share of the American market, this system has halted the process by which it was being displaced and has raised prices to the minimum required for survival of the Cuban industry.

In the world market, the disastrous Chadbourne plan, doomed to failure by its basic defects, was replaced in 1937 by the London sugar agreement. By including not only consumer countries but all the great exporters, the London agreement corrected the faults of the Chadbourne plan and assured the industry relative international stability, although it has not achieved entirely satisfactory price levels.

These international stabilization measures, largely brought about by the sustained and intelligent efforts of the Cuban sugar industry, are more pertinent to this study than it may appear. The obvious reason, as has already been pointed out, is that the economic and social problems created within the country by sugar production cannot be isolated from the industry's international position and policy. No matter how we may try at home to improve the situation of the farmers and workers and to enact more humane and just laws, we cannot succeed unless production is guaranteed a sound position in the world market.

REGULATION OF THE INDUSTRY

As we have stated, the sugar crisis, caused by a severe decline in exports, paralyzed latifundium expansion. In addition, it forced the sugar industry to take drastic steps to reduce production through zafra restrictions, which were first applied as a temporary measure and have become since 1930 an essential characteristic of Cuban sugar production.

Since zafras have been restricted to levels considerably lower than the industry's over-all capacity to produce, every manufacturing unit and agricultural zone has had to be held to limits based on international agreement, through a system of domestic regulation of production and export. Besides accomplishing this purpose, the system has also solved some of the industry's internal problems, especially those regarding relations between the manufacturing and the agricultural sectors, that is, between sugar mills and colonos.

Faced with the need to restrict zafras, the nation's first concern was how to carry out such a project. It was possible either to reduce production in proportion to the capacity of each factory and prorate the entire zafra among all the mills, or to guarantee a minimum number of bags to small mills in order to save them from ruin. Rules were finally adopted establishing a minimum production of 70,000 bags for small mills. This solution acknowledged the nation's desire to conserve mills and agricultural zones, to prevent concentration of production in the most highly competitive mills, and to disperse the sugar industry as widely as possible over Cuban territory.

This policy, which for the sake of the country went completely contrary to the "natural" process of survival of the fittest, has been maintained and reinforced by regulations in the industry. Without a doubt, it represents the triumph of national interest over the private interests of large corporations, and it is the guiding principle of the whole program of protection for colono and worker.

PROTECTION OF THE COLONO

As an inevitable consequence of protecting mills that would have been forced to shut down by free competition or prorated restrictions, cane agriculture was frozen in regions where it already existed. The system for regulating sugar output is organized to distribute and maintain production in agricultural regions that existed when the restriction program was initiated. It is designed to prevent the displacement of sugar mills and, even more important, of farms. It is guided by the principle of recognizing and respecting the rights of the interested parties in each zone: the manufacturing unit, the sugar mill; the colono, who has invested time and money there; the landowner, who realizes no income from his property unless cane is grown there; the worker, both industrial and agricultural, who earns his living there; the local storekeeper, who is supported by business based on sugar money; the transportation enterprises, which also depend on sugar for business; and, finally, the ayuntamiento, which receives from sugar mill and plantation most of the revenue it requires to operate its services.

Only the size, extent, and variety of these interests—no longer private, but part of a community—can justify keeping up sugar production in certain zones, which in practice if not in a legal sense prevents cane from being grown in other regions not designated as agricultural zones when restrictions were put into effect.

However, these regulations alone would not have protected the farmer. Now deprived of the relative advantage afforded him by competition among mills, he would have been in an even worse situation if other

measures had not come to his aid. Freezing cane production regions would not have prevented the substitution of administration farming for colono farming. The
process of latifundium absorption would have changed
its mode of operation, but the result for Cuba's rural
population and economic structure would have been the
same.

Even under the regulations, administration farming
could have gone on spreading and replacing the colono
by means of the old system of *colonos de pega*. These
so-called colonos were really straw men used by the
sugar mills to disguise administration farmers as
colonos.[1]

Protection for the colono has been made effective
through the "right of tenure," established in Article 26
of the Law of Sugar Coordination. It guarantees that
the colono may occupy and cultivate his land so long as
he grows enough cane to fill his quota and pays the rent
agreed upon or fixed by law. This means that the colono
may not be evicted from his holding for any other
reason.

But even this right, undoubtedly representing one of
the greatest gains of the colono group and the nation,
would nevertheless have been inadequate—in spite of
its broad and firm application by our courts of justice—
if it had not been supplemented by two other equally
fundamental measures: rent control and the setting of a

1. For confirmation of this point, see W. MacGaffey and C. R.
Barnett, *Cuba* (New Haven, HRAF Press, 1962), p. 42: "Some land
registered as colono-operated was actually managed by subsidiary
companies set up by the mills to take advantage of laws favoring
colonos over administration lands in the allocation of quotas."
[Editor's note.]

legal price for cane. It is easy to understand that the colono's right to remain on his land would have availed him very little if the mill had been free to offer him whatever amount it wished for his cane and thereby to limit the amount of rent he could pay. At the same time, even if the mill gave the colono a fair cash price for his cane, it could always have invalidated the effects of the law by regulating rents, since in most cases the mill was owner of the land which the colono farmed.

The price of cane has been fixed by the Law of Sugar Coordination, which assigned mill production to the farm sector in the following proportions:

1. When the mill's sugar yield does not exceed 12 per cent [of the raw cane], its equivalent in sugar of 48 per cent of such yield, not to exceed 5.75 arrobas, [is allotted to the colono].
2. When the mill's sugar yield is more than 12 per cent, but does not exceed 13 per cent, the equivalent in sugar of 47 per cent of such yield.
3. When the mill's sugar yield is more than 13 per cent, the equivalent in sugar of 46 per cent of such yield.

Since the average sugar yield in Cuba is approximately 1.5 per cent and the law allows the colono an additional 5 per cent of the yield when he farms his own land, it may be estimated that in general the number of arrobas of sugar allotted by the law is 52 per cent of sugar yield.

The average official price of warehouse sugar, which is used as a basis for payment of cane, is calculated every fifteen days by the Ministry of Agriculture, in accordance with specific provisions and in consultation with the Commission for Verification of Averages, made up of representatives of the mills, the colonos, and the government.

Rents have been regulated by the Law of Sugar Coordination, which, for purposes of payment, divides the farms into three areas. The first, designated as area A, is the amount of land on which enough cane is grown to meet the quota; the second, or area B, includes the land that completes the colony as a unit (roads, etc.); and area C is the rest of the controlled or uncontrolled land.

The rent of area C has not been regulated, and the terms are left to negotiation. If the rent agreed upon for area B is less than $15 a caballería, it may be raised to this figure. The law stipulates that rent payments for the principal area A, the cane fields, may not exceed $15 a caballería, when the land belongs to the mill. When the colono occupies land of his own or of a third party, the mill must pay the colono the price of cane and, in consideration of rent, an additional equivalent of 5 per cent of the sugar yield of the farm's cane that was ground during the zafra in question.

A final problem of the agricultural sector of the industry, that of agricultural credit, has had no official regulation. On the other hand, it could not have been regulated and solved by legal provisions. Its solution must be reached through economic and financial measures, by setting up the credit agencies needed to promote agricultural activities and to furnish easy credit not just to the colono but to the Cuban farmer in general.

Some progress recently has been made in this direction by creating a colono bank with an initial capital of two million pesos. It is run by the colonos themselves and is intended to satisfy the credit requirements of the cane farmer. The bank's only stockholders will be co-lonos, who may purchase its 200,000 shares at $10 each, on condition that no single stockholder may own more than 1 per cent of the bank's capital. This new institution merits the enthusiastic backing of the colono group because of its solid base, its limitations on finan-cial control, its founders, and, above all, its response to a deep and long-felt need.

CHANGES IN LABOR CONDITIONS

As regards the condition of the sugar worker and the change needed in the industry's labor relations, we should point out that nothing had been done about the importation of cheap laborers until it was absolutely and summarily prohibited by the new constitution. Despite the author's lack of confidence in the efficacy of legal and even constitutional provisions, he never-theless acknowledges that in this case the constitution fortunately terminated a situation created mainly by economic forces.

Now, for the first time in the industry's history, the sugar workers have powerful unions, through which they have been able to win adoption of a series of meas-ures assuring them a more equitable situation than they had during the period of latifundium domination. The institution of an eight-hour day in the mills, with the 24 hours of continuous operation divided into three shifts, has revolutionized this aspect of the industry by reducing the work day from 12 hours and increasing the number of workers by one-third.

Another change, just as far-reaching in the principle

it lays down if not in its immediate economic results, is the regulation of the wages of specialized and non-specialized factory and farm workers through a scale that varies with the price of sugar. Although this arrangement may not be entirely satisfactory, it nevertheless guarantees labor a minimum salary and a more elastic method of sharing in the country's prosperity.

Finally, sugar workers have received direct economic benefits from recognition of their right to organize and the systematic and firm enforcement of legal provisions giving them paid vacations, social security, and special wage increases to offset rises in the cost of living.[2]

To conclude this brief summary, we would like to make clear that even in the concrete aspects we have discussed above, the economic and social welfare of the affected sectors is still far from settled. We have deliberately avoided formulating an opinion about this for two reasons. First, because any analysis of the numerical results of a measure or situation involves factors that are difficult to estimate and examine objectively. Even if this were not true, consideration of the arroba or of wage scales from this standpoint would be of little use, since a change in the cost of cane production, in cane yield, or in the worker's cost of living, would invalidate the analysis.

Second, the foregoing leads us to believe that the only effective way to correct the maladjustments caused by varying circumstances is to establish invariable princi-

2. Law No. 20 of March 21, 1941, set up a fund for retirement and social security for employees and workers of the sugar industry. It was implemented by Decree 3383 of Nov. 16, 1943, which guaranteed a pension to all the industry's employees and workers after the ages of 55 and 70. The industry contributes a substantial part of this fund.

ples to guide reform measures. Then it will be possible
to eliminate injustices, carry out the necessary reforms
peaceably, and gradually restore the Cuban sugar farmer and worker to their rightful place in society.

THE REMAINING PROBLEMS

Cuba's remaining economic and social problems can
be reduced to two important and pervasive ones: the
continued concentration of cane agriculture and the
long duration of the dead season, with the consequent
mass unemployment of the almost half-million farm
and industrial workers. Although both are far-reaching
problems, they are very different. The first is fundamentally a question of organization and can, therefore,
be solved at once through appropriate economic legislation. The second, however, is essentially a question of
creating, promoting, and developing new activities to
provide employment to the enormous labor force left
idle at the end of every zafra.

An idea of the magnitude of the first problem may be
grasped from the fact that the 1,171 colono farms, each
of which produces more than 500,000 arrobas of cane
(considering for this purpose as colono farms those administered by the mills, which make up 3.9 per cent of
the total), in 1937 grew 1,998,229,000 arrobas of cane,
or 55.03 per cent of all the cane grown in Cuba that
year. On the other hand, the 17,717 small colonos who
have the right to grind up to 30,000 arrobas and who
make up 59.01 per cent of all the colono group, grew
318,463,834 arrobas, or only 8.76 per cent of the total.
The rest of the cane, equaling 36.20 per cent, was
grown by the remaining 37.08 per cent of the colono

group, who produce between 30,000 and 50,000 arrobas each. We see that 3.9 per cent of the colonos produce more than half the cane, while 59 per cent produce only a meager 8 per cent.

The concentration of cane agriculture is even more clearly revealed by noting that if all cane were allocated at the rate of 30,000 arrobas to each colono, there would be more than 121,000 cane farmers in Cuba, instead of the present 30,020. And the great majority of farmers who now own very little cane would realize a substantial income from their increased quotas. We present this calculation simply to illustrate the problem, not because we believe it suggests a direct solution for Cuba.

In brief, cane concentration means that a relatively small number of growers benefit from the only agricultural activity in Cuba that offers the farmer a fluctuating but fairly sure income today.

Despite the fact that the cane grower's income varies with the volume of the zafra and the price of sugar— forces practically beyond control—the Cuban farmer who is protected by a quota for his cane has a considerable advantage over the farmer who raises cane under the same conditions but is not protected. Cuba's climate is so favorable that a general crop failure is almost unknown, and sugar always has a ready market at a price set by the government.

The farmer who has been allotted a quota of, let us say, 30,000 arrobas of cane and who works his land with the aid of his sons is guaranteed an income that enables him to buy food, clothing, and whatever else he needs and cannot produce on his farm. This quota, at an average price for sugar of 1.5 cents a pound, gives the farmer an income of 731 pesos. The price of this year's zafra brought him an annual income of 1,200 pesos, or100 pesos a month. No other farm crop that he would market would yield him so high and steady an income. When these proceeds are combined with his truck gardening for family consumption and sale, the cane farmer we describe earns considerably more than the rural family whose cane is not protected by a quota, not to mention the one who grows no cane at all.

In addition to high income, the cane quota offers another significant advantage. Under present conditions in Cuban agriculture, and precisely because no other crop has so dependable a harvest and sale, a farmer cannot rent a piece of land in any part of the island unless he possesses a cane quota, which guarantees that the landowner will be paid his rent.

This situation gives rise to a serious problem for the farmer who lives with his family on provision grounds, whether or not he grows cane. When his sons reach manhood, there is no land available for them to settle on, and they must either remain single or establish their new households on the same farm. In the first case, the increase in rural population is checked and the promotion of agriculture is paralyzed; new generations of farmers are plunged into despair and pessimism. In the second case, the farm is burdened with more people than it can support, which lowers the living standard of all its occupants.

Obviously, these are problems that will prevent Cuba's rural population from making any progress. Until new agricultural activities are found and developed, Cuba is threatened with the stagnation and steady impoverishment of the real source of its vitality.

REGIONAL REGULATION OF CANE PRODUCTION

It must be remembered that many of the administered cane plantations in Camagüey and Oriente were not originally farmed by colonos and later taken over by the latifundium. In certain regions the large plantations are the necessary consequence of building sugar mills in deserted areas where there is still not enough rural population to carry on small-scale agriculture. This difficulty and others that we are unable to go into here indicate that any solution will have to be undertaken gradually.

A policy of regional regulation will benefit the country's economy in many ways. It will raise the living standard and purchasing power of the rural population, thereby expanding the domestic market. As a result, it will make possible the development of other branches of agriculture and national industry. Moreover, if regional regulation is conducted so that it does not upset the sugar industry, it will strengthen, not weaken, the latter's structure by increasing its resistance to periods of low prices. In this respect, the small farmer is vastly superior to the plantation operated as an industrial enterprise, because his final concern is simply physical survival.

To some extent, regional regulation of the industry would be greatly facilitated since the industry has already created an efficient mechanism for its own regulation, which was made necessary by the controls and restrictions on sugar exports.[3] Separation of a given

3. The author is probably referring to certain restrictions favoring the independent colono over the latifundium as cane-growers. It was these restrictions which led to the creation of colonos on paper, in areas where the cane was in fact produced by the central. [Editor's note.]

percentage of all cane grown under the quota system might be accomplished by taking it from farms that exceed a certain limit, or from administered farms. From this reserve, quotas of 30,000 arrobas might be allotted to farmers who meet specifiable requirements, for example, Cuban nationality and personal occupancy and management of their farms; and preference might be given to farmers with families when the children live and work on their fathers' farms.

In the present legislation, which has established a fund to protect the small colono, the principle of this measure is recognized, and the method suggested for its application is accepted, at least in a very narrow sense. Now it is essentially a question of extending its principle not only to grant increases to colonos who have low grinding quotas, but to create new colonos. In this way, it may become a powerful instrument for wider distribution of agrarian wealth and reinforcement of the economic and social organization and, ultimately, of the sugar industry itself.

THE PROBLEM OF THE DEAD SEASON

In our opinion, the mass unemployment caused every year by the dead season, a problem so well known that it needs no explanation, may be attacked through two different programs. One, which would be long term and broader in scope, would depend mainly on private enterprise. It would be devoted to finding, encouraging, and developing new productive activities connected with the sugar industry that would prolong the period of operation. For this purpose, the by-products of sugar manufacture offer immediate possibilities, which we shall discuss briefly. The other would be a colonization program to settle field workers as farmers on plots of land within or around sugar plantations. These subsistence farms could supply food to the rural working population and thereby raise the total real income.

The production of high-grade molasses, on the increase since 1937, is a shining example of how by-products can raise the total volume of the zafra and prolong its duration. Unfortunately, up to now the export trade in molasses, principally used in the manufacture of industrial alcohol in the United States, is entirely controlled by three or four subsidiaries of American distilleries. These companies, anticipating the rise in Cuba's output of molasses, have kept prices very low. Consequently, both the cane and labor used in its production have been paid for at a rate far below that of the sugar zafra.

We do not believe this means that the effort has failed in its objective. It simply indicates that molasses should no longer be produced exclusively for export, but should be made the basis of a national industry. Without going into the technical details, we have reason to believe that a domestic fuel industry can be built on the ready, cheap, and abundant supply of molasses. Also, flour for use in scientifically balanced livestock feed is another very promising by-product of sugar cane, and it would assist in expanding our exports of live cattle and refrigerated meat to the huge United States market. With Cuba's excellent pasture land, cattle herds, and proximity to the United States, it is ideally situated to develop an important livestock industry, if the quality of the beef can be improved. This depends to some extent on the breeds themselves, but even more on fattening cattle economically on balanced feed so that their meat will be of the type preferred by the American consumer.

Cuba also has the necessary raw materials for feed manufacture. Numerous tests have demonstrated the incomparable advantages of livestock feed made from mixing cane flour—just ground sugar cane—with pea-nut-oil cake. It would be simple and inexpensive to set up in different regions small plants to produce this superior feed, which is prepared without any imported materials. Since, in addition, large herds of cattle are owned by mills, it is easy to appreciate the value of promoting this activity to supplement the sugar zafra.

Finally, without going into the chemical by-products that might be developed by the sugar industry, I would like to mention the possibilities offered by the processing of bagasse. Every year thousands of different articles are being made of plastic: electrical appliances and parts, radios, bottle caps, inkwells, fountain pens, table tops, ashtrays, etc. In bagasse, of which thousands of tons are left over from every zafra, we have a magnificent source of high-grade, economical plastics material, better and cheaper than many of those now manufactured. With the material cheaply produced in Cuba, it is easy to imagine not only how many industries might be based on plastic manufacture, but also their export possibilities.

FARM COLONIZATION

The second of the two possible solutions to the serious problem of seasonal unemployment is to provide land to the field laborers which can be farmed by them during the dead season. There is nothing new in the idea of settling agricultural workers on plots of land where they can grow garden crops. It was suggested by the American Commission of the Foreign Policy Association which visited Cuba in 1934, and several attempts along this line have been made in different parts of the country.

The United Fruit Company, which owns both cane and banana plantations in Oriente, several years ago tried to move families of that province to homes built on farm sections of its own property. Although we do not know exactly what happened, the experiment did not succeed and the farms were rapidly vacated. We believe it failed because subsistence farms in cane-growing regions can only be settled permanently if the transient field hands who return year after year to work in the zafras of a given mill have adequate reason to remain. Colonizing enterprises that offer no more than provision grounds cannot attract rural families in search of additional income to raise their standard of living.

In our opinion, the effects of farm colonization can never be very widespread or complete. Sooner or later it will be necessary to work out a more equitable distribution of cane cultivation as a solution to the problem of seasonal unemployment, as well as the equally important problem of labor shortage in certain areas.

Nonetheless, despite the partial and limited aspect of this proposal, such measures are demanded by the scarcity of workers available to some mills and to large colonos and by the government law that obliges sugar centrales to plant basic food crops. Since it can no longer count on cheap labor from the other islands, the sugar industry must find a way to assure itself of an adequate local labor force. And, if the government really encourages diversified agriculture and insists on participation by the sugar industry, it will have taken an important step toward providing workers with steady employment by establishing a need for permanent crop farmers.

If the two problems of concentration of cane agriculture and seasonal unemployment can be solved—and the obstacles are not unsurmountable—we shall have made great progress. We must halt the latifundium process, give the colono security, adopt measures to guarantee that the worker will be protected and his situation improved, distribute cane agriculture more widely, and utilize by-products to shorten the dead season and reinforce and supplement sugar production. Once these objectives are attained, the Cuban sugar industry will represent a truly fruitful occupation, constituted on principles that afford maximum benefit to the country, correct the serious deficiencies caused by so many sugar crises, and coordinate the principal source of our foreign exchange with other existing and developing productive activities. Then we shall be prepared to return to a task that was interrupted and almost terminated by the latifundium catastrophe. Using whatever means necessary, we can work slowly toward giving Cuba back its land and its national identity.

Appendix 2.
Model Contract

This contract for colonos was submitted to a group of them by a powerful sugar company that owns several mills in the province of Oriente. Because of protests on the part of the colonos, a few minor details of the contract were modified. Essentially, however, it is the standard contract entered into by the colono and represents the viewpoint of the latifundium company. It clearly demonstrates that when we described the colono as an economic vassal subjected to a purely feudal system, we were not using a figure of speech, but were speaking literally and precisely.

CENTRAL ...., ORIENTE, REPUBLIC OF CUBA,

ON ...., 19....

CONTRACT COVERING AGRICULTURAL FINANCING, SUGAR CANE FARMING, AND MILLING

Contracting Parties

....

....

....

First. Definition of the boundaries of the property.
Second. That the party of the first part has agreed with the party of the second part, the colono, to enter into a contract covering agricultural financing, sugar cane farming and milling, which is subject to the following

Provisions

1. The Company gives to the colono for farming the land known as ...., which forms part of the plantation described in the first clause of the contract, and which is described as follows: [Description of the land forming the object of this contract.]

The colono acknowledges full ownership of the cane shoots, cane, yards, buildings, farm implements, and other present and future improvements and products of the farm described, which has an area of approximately .... caballerías devoted to the cultivation of sugar cane and the rest to pasture grounds, yards, wagon roads, and other properties of the farm. The colono guarantees that the sole lien on this farm is its debt to the company.

2. The Company reserves to itself absolute owner-ship of the land described in the preceding paragraph (1), and the colono, in rental of this land, will pay an-nually to the Company the sum of 100 pesos, legal tender, per caballería. The colono will pay this sum in yearly amounts due on March 31 of each year in the office of the Central. The colono specifically renounces the right granted to him in Article 1.575 of the Civil Code to request a reduction in his rental, in case of an act of God.

3. The colono is obliged to devote all the land form-ing the object of this contract to the cultivation of sugar cane, except for that part which he must reserve for intermediate paths or wagon roads, pasture grounds, mill yards, buildings, or food crops (with the exception of sorghum corn or any other plant that is detrimental to cane farming), and other purposes necessary to the promotion and maintenance of the farm.

4. The Company reserves the right to fix the extent of the land that, under the preceding paragraph (3), the colono must devote to each purpose.

5. The colono is obligated to maintain the cane fields in the best possible condition and to keep fences and buildings in good repair. The colono also must destroy diseased cane and harmful weeds or plants such as the "Don Carlos" weed and the "Marabú" plant. In case the colono fails to do what in the Company's judgment is necessary, the Company itself will carry out, at the colono's expense, what it considers necessary.

6. When he sows new cane, the colono shall use exclusively seeds that are not infected with the mosaic

or any other disease and that are of the type known as "crystalline" or any other variety designated by the Company. The colono expressly recognizes the Company's right to inspect seeds before planting. The Company shall also have the right to inspect fields and destroy all cane infected with the mosaic or any other disease, and the colono shall replant at his own expense, using healthy seeds of the type or types indicated by the Company.

7. The Company shall at all times have the right, expressly recognized by the colono, to send its employees to inspect the farm; to cross the land which forms the object of this contract and to build thereon railroad lines and open passage for any kind of vehicle whatsoever that the Company deems necessary to its own or another's interest; to construct roads and dig ditches in any direction that it may consider advisable; and to utilize any wood, water, sand, stone, or other similar materials that there may be in the farm, and the colono shall extend to the Company every facility for carrying out whatever is agreed upon in this clause.

8. Unless written permission is granted by the Company, the colono shall not establish or permit the establishment of rights of way or roads of any kind in favor of any person or entity, in the land forming the object of this contract.

9. If the Company, making use of the right reserved to it in paragraph (7) of this contract, should have to destroy cane shoots, fences, or other improvements made by the colono, it will pay the latter their fair value; but the Company shall not reduce the colono's rent in proportion to the extent of land that it occupies when it makes use of its right, if the road, highway, or railroad

constructed by the Company, in its opinion, compensates the colono for the use of his land.

10. The Company, making use of the right reserved to it in paragraph (7), may establish scales and transfer cars to weigh and load the sugar cane of the colono or other colonos; and neither the Company nor the colonos will be required to pay for more than the cane shoots or improvements that are destroyed in the process of installing such equipment, and for the damage done by the operators of this equipment.

11. Under the terms of the present contract, all sugar cane that is grown on the land forming the object of this contract and that the Company considers to be well-ripened and ready for grinding, shall be sold and delivered on railroad cars by the colono to the Company, to be ground during the zafra periods in the Central .... or in the mill designated by the Company. Such sugar cane must be carefully stacked, free from straw, roots, and shoots, and it must be of the type known as "crystalline," specified in paragraph (6) or any other variety approved by the Company. With permission of the Company, the colono may reserve for himself some of the cane for seeds.

12. The Company agrees to buy and receive on railroad cars all the cane that under the preceding paragraph (11) the colono must deliver, to be ground in the Central .... or in the mill designated by the Company.

13. The Company shall advise the colono, by means of a circular letter ten days beforehand, the date on which he should begin cutting his cane, and the latter is obliged to begin cutting on the date fixed by the Company. It will do the colono no good to argue that he did

not receive the letter, if it has been sent to all the colonos.

14. The Company agrees that during the grinding period of the mill, it will provide every day in the chucho of .... or in the one that it considers most convenient, unless prevented by some force beyond its control, the number of cars that it deems necessary for loading the cane to be delivered by the colono. The amount of cane to be delivered daily during the zafra by each farm will be determined by the Company according to its appraisal of the cane grown in all the farms. The Company will begin to supply the cars referred to in this clause two days after the date set for cutting. The number of cars to be allocated to each farm will be calculated from the date that the first cars are supplied.

15. If the colono fails to begin cutting and to deliver his cane on the dates set for him and under the terms agreed to in this contract, the Company will have the right to do this at the colono's expense, and the latter may not intervene with the Company for any reason in the cutting and milling of his cane, all of which the colono hereby accepts.

16. The sugar cane delivered by the colono will be paid for on the basis of its weight as indicated by the scale of the mill yard of the plantation where it is ground, and the colono may check this weight personally, or through a delegate, as often as may be reasonable, at his own expense.

17. Payments for cane delivered by the colono will be made at approximately two-week intervals, during the first ten days of the fortnight following the date of delivery.

18. For every hundred arrobas of cane that the co-

lono delivers to the Company, as agreed in paragraphs (11), (16), and (17), the Company will pay the colono the value in official currency of five and a quarter (5¼) arrobas of centrifugal sugar, with juice of a polarization of 96 degrees, according to the average price for the fifteen-day period during which the cane was ground, as quoted by the Association of Havana Sugar Brokers or by the agency or entity that legally replaces or amends it. But in any case, the Company will pay the colono, as a minimum price, the amount of two pesos and twenty-five cents, in Cuban currency, for every hundred arrobas of cane delivered, although the average price quoted may be less.

19. The colono is obliged to cut the cane to the level of the ground and to replant bare patches in the cut fields.

20. There will be charged to the colono's account all the expenses of cultivation, cutting, loading, hauling, stacking, and other sugar cane operations, until it is loaded onto the railroad cars.

21. In case the colono's sugar cane is burnt and he is not held responsible, the Company will make no deduction from the established price, during the first three days following the fire, if there is no rain. After this period, or before then if there is rain, the Company will decide whether or not to grind the burnt cane, and should it decide to do so, will fix a price for such cane. The Company, as long as there is burnt cane, agrees to increase the number of railroad cars to as many as it may consider necessary to assign to that farm.

22. The colono is obliged to give all necessary assistance to other colonos of the region in case of fire. He will make available, at the current prices of the

region, his employees, his mill yards, and his carts, not only to extinguish the fire rapidly, but to cut and cart the burnt cane.

23. Under no circumstances may the colono burn woodland, cane, weeds, straw, rubbish, or other materials within the farm, without the written authorization of the Company, which he should request at least two days in advance. Once he has received this authorization, he should carry out such burning in accordance with the instructions of the Company. In any case, whatever damages and losses may be caused by such burnings, whether to the Company or to a third party, will be duly indemnified by the colono.

24. In no case will the Company be obliged to indemnify the colono for any damage that the latter may suffer due to a delay in the delivery of railroad cars, a standstill or interruption in the grinding of the sugar, a carry-over of the farm's cane at the end of the zafra because it could not be ground, or to any other cause; but the Company will do everything possible in every case to prevent the colono from suffering damage, and in the event of a prolonged interruption in the grinding, or if the mill completes its zafra, the Company will make every effort to sell the colono's cane to another Central.

25. The colono acknowledges, declares, and recognizes that he is indebted to the Company in the amount of .... pesos in Cuban currency for advances and loans made to him prior to ...., 19...., by the Company for the promotion, planting, cultivation, administration, and general maintenance of said farm, described in paragraph (1), including interest accrued to the date indicated.

26. The colono agrees to repay said amount in the same currency, excluding all other money or scrip in place thereof, to the Company, in the office of the Central, in the following manner: .... per cent, or the amount of .... pesos on ...., 19 ..., etc.

Moreover, the colono at any time may make partial payments on the principal owed, but such partial payments will not liquidate his debt.

27. The colono is obliged to pay in cash to the Company interest at the rate of *8 per cent* per annum on all or that part of the principal owed by him, in the office of the Central; but he will never be charged as interest on arrears a sum exceeding the total annual payment due.

Said interest will be paid in annual installments, due on March 31 of each year and any sum collected by the Company by reason of this contract will be first applied to payment of the interest, and then to the principal.

28. Failure to meet payments of the interest or principal on any of the stipulated dates, or failure to fulfill any of the conditions of this contract, will give the Company the right to initiate foreclosure proceedings for the net amount of the principal and interest and the expenses and costs that are owed to it. The amount of the principal owed under paragraph (27) plus accrued interest will be claimed by the Company without affecting its obligation to credit and deduct in its suit as fair and legitimate payments the sums that it may have collected in payment of principal, interest, repayment, or any other purpose in connection with the present loan; and it is agreed expressly that the amount determined in the suit be considered in every case the net balance, and that any error or difference may only be claimed in a

separate suit or considered as a legitimate deductible payment.

29. The colono creates a preferential lien in the Company's favor of all the cane shoots and cane, present and future products or assets of said farm from ...., 19...., to ...., 19...., in accordance with the stipulations of the law of March 2, 1922, in order to guarantee the principal and interest and also an additional amount of .... pesos for expenses and costs.

30. Without affecting the terms of this contract, the Company, if it considers it to be in the best interests of the farm, and as a guarantee of its investment, reserves the right to advance to the colono, in cash, a part of the price agreed upon for the cane to be delivered by the colono, under the following conditions: (a) The amounts that the Company advances to the colono will be exclusively devoted to the sowing, cultivation, administration, and other expenses of the farm, setting as a maximum for this credit the sum of 1000 pesos a year, in Cuban currency, for each caballería included in the land forming the object of this contract, as described in paragraph (1), but at no moment shall the advances outstanding exceed said maximum sum for each caballería, plus a year of interest, or 1080 pesos. (b) The Company will charge the colono 8 per cent interest a year on these advances, during the entire period that they are outstanding. (c) These advances to the colono shall be recorded in a notarized receipt or in private receipts, one of the copies of which the Company may register or deposit with a notary public.

31. The colono cedes irrevocably to the Company until the contract expires, and as long as the debts incurred by reason of this contract are outstanding, the

right to take possession of the sums produced by the cane shoots and cane which the colono put up as collateral, and these sums will be credited by the Company to the colono's account. The Company will also be authorized to file the corresponding notices and to ask that this ceding of property be entered into the Property Registry where this contract is recorded.

In no case shall the Company's receipt of such sums by reason of this transfer have the effect of making the debt irrecoverable, without affecting the Company's already stated obligation to credit and recognize legitimate payments.

32. The Company, when it makes use of the right given to it by the preceding clause (31) and when it carries out its settlements every fifteen days, will make the following distribution when it credits the colono in the official books: (a) advances for cutting and hauling; (b) interest on other advances; (c) principal of other advances; (d) repayment of the agricultural loan under the following terms. If the debt of the colono with the Company is less than 1000 pesos per caballería of shoots in good condition, it will give to the colono 50 per cent of the net balance in cash, after making the above deductions, and will credit the rest toward the repayment of interest and principal. If the colono's debt to the Company exceeds 1000 pesos per caballería, the Company will retain all the rest of the settlement, after making the above deductions, for the repayment of interest and principal.

33. In the event of the colono's death or incapacity, or if for any other reason he is unable to administer the farm, or if he should cease to live on the farm, the Company will have the right to designate immediately an

administrator for said farm, so that the latter may take charge of all the work, and all expenses incurred by the Company or the administrator during this period will be for the account of and payable by the colono.

34. In the event of nonfulfillment by the colono of any of the obligations stipulated by this contract, the Company will be entitled, separately or jointly, to take action to attach the farm or other assets of the debtor. The Company may, without affecting any other rights it may enjoy, request in its suit the judicial administration of the farm in these cases, as well as in any of the other cases referred to in Article 12 of the law of March 2, 1922, without need to put up security of any kind, and it will only be obligated to credit to the account of the colono all the net profits that it earns by administration of the farm.

35. The Company may cede or endorse this contract without knowledge of the colono, but the colono cannot cede, lease, or transfer in any way or encumber the farm or any part of it to a third party or entity, without written consent of the Company, and in the event that a third person should be assigned by the court to administer the farm or for any cause whatsoever a party other than the colono should administer it, the Company will be authorized to declare all loans due and initiate foreclosure proceedings.

36. The colono is obliged to deliver to the Company and to sign any document or deed that the Registrar of Property may require to record the present contract, or correct errors, or improve or confirm any title or contract which it may be necessary to record or enter.

37. In no case will the colono be allowed to establish or to permit the establishment of any business in

the farm, without the written consent of the Company. Eating establishments for the workers of the farm are excepted.

38. On termination of this contract, in the event that one of the parties should not wish to extend it, or if the Company, because of nonfulfillment of said contract by the colono, should make use of the right granted it by said contract to take possession of the farm, then all the farm's improvements, including buildings, workers' lodgings, fences, cane shoots, and fruits of every kind, shall be for the exclusive benefit of the Company, which will pay the colono the value of said improvements in the following manner: The farm will be appraised, with the exception of materials and buildings not necessary to the development of the farm. This appraisal will be carried out by two experts, one of them appointed by the colono and the other by the Company. If these two experts should not reach an agreement, a third one will be appointed and his appraisal will be accepted by all. These experts should be appointed within five days after the date on which either one of the parties has been notified officially by the other party that he desires such appointments to be made. In the event that one of the parties should not appoint an expert within the determined period, it will be presumed that he is in agreement with the appointment of the other party's expert, who will be authorized to make his appraisal alone. In no case will thatched huts be valued at more than 50 pesos each, and the workers' lodgings at more than 2500 pesos each. The Company and the colono agree that in no case will the Company accept the appraisal of more than one lodging house in each colono farm, although the colono may have built others for his con-

venience, unless such lodging houses are authorized in writing by the Company. The Company will reimburse the colono 75 per cent of the amount of this appraisal, and will reserve for itself the remaining 25 per cent. If the colono should owe the Company more than the amount covered by 75 per cent of the appraised value, the Company reserves the right to take over the oxen, carts, and other assets of the colono until the debt is covered.

39. This contract will expire after six years or zafras, which will date from ...., 19...., to ...., 19...., and it may be extended for .... years, at option of the Company, if the colono agrees.

40. This contract will be recorded in the Property Registry of .... and it will be canceled on the date of its expiration. In all cases referred to in Article 26 of the law of March 2, 1922, except as provided for in Article 13 and Paragraph 4 of Article 28 of said law, it will also be canceled. In cases where cancellation of the contract may take place earlier by reason of the maturity of the loan, the Company, if it so desires, may request and obtain such cancellation.

41. This contract is private and, therefore, the colono is not permitted to transfer, cede, encumber or exchange in any form the rights that he acquires under said contract, without the express and written consent of the Company, for which purpose he hereby renounces the rights granted him by the law of agricultural credit of March 2, 1922, Paragraph (D), Article 16.

42. In any of the cases stipulated in this contract that authorize the Company to terminate its obligation, legal action shall be taken by this fact alone, without

affecting the responsibility it may incur for malice or negligence in the facts it alleges for the purpose of instituting legal action.

43. The colono will be charged with all expenses relative to this contract and legal costs including fees of lawyers used by the Company, in the event that the colono is the cause of the action, and he will also be charged with the registration fees, and with all kinds of fees, taxes, and present and future taxes on this contract, and on the loan hereunder extended. The Company shall collect the amount of the loan and interest, clear of encumbrance.

44. The colono states that he accepts the terms of the present contract covering agricultural financing, sugar cane farming, and milling and that he binds himself to fulfill its conditions, hereby authorizing the Company to make use of the rights that it reserves for itself, if he should be unable to or for any reason should fail to fulfill the agreement.

45. The colono, as long as the contract is in force, agrees not to request or accept from third parties or entities loans for maintenance or amounts secured by the farm which is the object of this contract, or by its properties or present or future products, without the express and written consent of the Company. In the event that this contract should not be fulfilled and that some creditor should sue for his loan, the colono authorizes the Company to take possession of the farm and declare this contract to be terminated.

46. Both parties expressly renounce the jurisdiction corresponding to their domicile and, as regards the carrying out of any legal or extralegal proceedings, as

well as the determination of any difference that might arise due to this contract, designate for such purposes the judges and courts of the city of ....

In witness thereof, the contracting parties sign duplicate copies in the presence of the following witnesses, who are of age and residents of ...., who also sign with the contracting parties.

....

Colono   *By power of attorney*

....

Witness   *Witness*

Glossary

arroba	25.35 pounds or 11.50 kilograms
audiencia	in Spanish America, highest royal court of appeal in a district municipal government
ayuntamiento	municipal government
bozal	"unseasoned" African slave, just imported
caballería	a land measure of 33.16 acres or 13.42 hectares
cabildo	municipal corporation
cachimbo	small sugar mill
central	large-scale sugar cane grinding mill, of the sort developed in Cuba after 1880
chucho	railroad station for cane loading
comunero	proprietor of a joint hacienda
colono	small farmer. The term *colono* in its simplest meaning refers to the "small-scale farmer." However, in most instances it is used

to describe a cultivator of sugar cane specifically. Furthermore, the term was expanded in the nineteenth century in Cuba, when the cultivation of cane became separated to some extent from its processing. Thereupon independent cane-growers entered into contractual grinding agreements with particular mills to which they delivered their cane when it was cut. Normally, such colonos owned their own land. Soon a new practice developed by which the central (mill), which had large tracts of owned or rented land, contracted with landless individual farmers, by what were essentially sharecropping or tenant arrangements, to grow cane. Thus a colono can be a small-scale farmer, a landowning sugar cane farmer who has a grinding contract with a mill, or a tenant producing cane on land owned or rented by the mill.

colono de pega   a false colono; one used by a latifundium to cloak corporate operation of cane farms

ejido   municipal commons

estancia   in Cuba, a small farm

guajiro	the Cuban countryman or rural dweller
guarapo	cane juice
hacendado	mill owner
hacienda	plantation; ranch; estate
hacienda comunera	a hacienda with several owners
hato	cattle ranch
indio encomendado	Indian serf or estate laborer
latifundium	the large, corporation-owned land and factory sugar combine
muscovado	brown, unrefined sugar
pesos de posesión	share in a hacienda comunera
realenga	unappropriated land belonging to the king
juicio de residencia	judicial review of an official's conduct at the end of his term
subpuerto	private coastal pier
tiempo muerto	literally, "dead time." The slack period during which there is no sugar cane harvest
zafra	cane harvesting and grinding period

Index